HUMAN RESOURCE RESOURCE TRAINING HOW IMPROVES

ORGANIZATIONAL PERFORMANCE

JOHN LOK

Copyright © John Lok
All Rights Reserved.

Contents

PREFACE

Summary

This book concerns how to apply how behavioral economic and psychological methods to attempt to explain whether your organization can be influenced to raise your employee individual productive efficiency as well as improve service performance to achieve to let your clients feel more satisfaction by effective human resource training or/and facility management methods. My research questions include: Can effective human resource training program improve your organization's employee individual skill level in order to raise productive efficiency and/or service performance?

I shall apply psychological method to attempt to recommend whether it is the right time to your organization ought need to find methods to raise your organization's human resource trai8ning course(s) quality and/or improve your organization's facility management in-house service quality to let your employees feel more comfortable to work in your organization's any working environment in order to achieve the raising productive efficiency and/or improving service performance consequence in possible.

This book indicates to explain whether effective human resource training courses can help to raise employee productive efficiency and/or improve service performance. I shall indicate the whole HRM successful elements to explain whether it can still help the organization to raise employee efficiency and/or improve service performance, if the organization neglects to implement an effective human resource training course program to let whose employees to attempt to learn any work-related skills.

The challenges of the HR specialist when there engage in attempt of increasing the individual and organization performances in Multinational companies through developing a set of HRM best practices, especially relating to employee recruitment and selection, performance management and staff retention. Since the organizations are multinational number of concerns are arises such as dealing cultural issues with the organizational goals as well as individual goals.

Furthermore organizational prehaviors and tools such as engagement, motivation and empowerment are basically highlighted; without those it is merely a dream to achieving the business goals. Basically Multinational companies are aiming profits and there for individual and organization performance are very vital for their existence.HR has been organized in a different ways over the years. Some functions have emphasized delivery by location or by business structure.

This book explains why human resource strategy can bring organizational benefits. It will explain how reward strategy can bring what kinds of benefits to organizations. Reward management is nowadays considered as an important topic in order to achieve the goals of a company. Employees are considered as the main factor which plays an important role in the organization. The success of each and every organization is its dedicated employee's .Current world is filled with changes and competition. In order to survive in the current situation companies should be having employees who are loyal and expert in their own field. New technologies are developed constantly and the companies are eagerly trying to catch up those talented employees with right expertise in their own areas. So, fair award management can attract talented employees to choose the organization to work.

When the organization has good reward management, then it will bring good organizational development, good learning and training , good performance management, good sourcing and staff, good employee engagement. In my this book, I shall explain how and why good reward management will bring all above these any one of human resource related issues to let readers to make accurate and reasonable analysis.

PROLOGUE

Table of content

Chapter One
Training how to impact of workplace
management on well-being and
productivity

Chapter Two
Organizational environment factor
influences the new employees
production efficiencies

Chapter Three
Interview psychology methods

What are common psychology methods of
recruitment choice?
Why does need to test the applicant's
psychological behavior in the
interview process?

How to apply psychological recruitment
strategies effect/manage in the
recruitment process?
How to apply occupational psychological
test method to test applicant's ability?

How selection assessment methods are applied to choose the best applicants ?

How to criteria for selecting and evaluating assessment methods in interview?

Reference

Chapter Four

Employee satisfaction measurement

● How to measure employee satisfaction ?

● How can leaders satisfy employee needs? p.46-60

● How does one company raise employee efficiency

Chapter Five

Organizational behavior theory

● What is system approach? p.61-77

Employee satisfaction methods

● How can satisfy to employees' needs?

● How to achieve work motivation strategy ?

● How can influence organizational positive behaviors ?

Reference

Chapter Six

How to learn qualified research interviewing in order to raise efficiency and effectiveness

● Psychological methods predict employee individual productive efficiency and service performance

Chapter Four

How to apply psychological methods to predict employee individual productive efficiency and service performance

● Aims and hypotheses in employee performance psychological research p.78-85

● What are variables, concepts and
measures meaning to any employee
performance psychological research p.86-94

I

Training how to impact of workplace management on well-being and productivity

In facility management strategy, design can lead promotion, the value of offices that are enriched, particularly including warehouses, shopping centers to raise their market value. Moreover, effective organizations, such as raising powering workers when giving the effective design of office space. I assume that a good design of an interior office workspace environment seems a psychological department to influence staff individual emotion to bring positive power in order to raising productive efficient influence, such as in a commercial city office. So, it brings this question: How workspace management strategy can impact on staff's working behaviors in office.

In fact, office tasks general include various forms of productivity, e.g. information processing, information management and any clerical tasks by computerization. Hence, office productivity concerns how to influence each office white color worker applies computers to work in office. The office space can impact on white color workers' performances in these several aspects: feeling of psychological comfort, organizational physical comfort and job satisfaction and productivity, efficiency. So, it seems that office workspace design strategy can influence white color workers' working behavior and attitude and performance indirectly.

The office space management includes: how to removal from the workspace of everything except the materials required to do the job at hand, how tight managerial control of the workspace, and how to implement standardization of managerial practice and workspace design. So, these key ideas will influence how each white color worker's efficiency and productivity in office working environment.

For this office space design situation, a large unseparated small space size's space design can accommodate more people and so brings itself to economies of scale. As a result, space occupancy can be centrally managed with minimal disruptive interference from office workers. Indeed, many businesses now adopt a clean and fresh air office working policy because they have more employees than they have spaces at which they can work. This desks are either taken on a first -come first -served basis. (hot desking) or can be booked in advance. So , when a company has many employees need to work in a small space working environment. It must concern how to let staffs to feel more comfortable in order to reduce high psychological pressure to work in this uncomfortable working environment. Hence, it explains why workspace design can impact on office workers' performance in some offices. All these issues are assumed that empowering workers to manage and have input into the design of their own workspace, then the effective office or any working places space management will enhance wellbeing to bring workers' positive emotions and improving productivity. I also assume the space working environment design have relationship of these depend variable factors to influence office worker individual productive efficiency. The variable factors may include psychological comfort, organizational comfortable, job satisfaction, physical comfort and productivity.

However, office furniture , facilities will influence office white color workers' performance ,e.g. the room size whether is big or small for manage office worker, a high backed, comfortable leather chair is needed for office staffs to sit down to let more comfortable, the door and most of the walls need glass, the office room environment needs have sea-grass rug beneath the desk covering the immediate working area, the office also needs have plants and pictures, mail boxes, telephone and computer facility is needed. When one staff needs to send email or phone call or send letters or deliver documents conveniently. These office elements are essential in order to increase physical well-being and feeling of satisfaction to white-color workers. Hence, geren office and office working space design management is needed in order to influence white color workers' productive efficiency in long term.

● Effective workspace design can influence communication to raise productivity

Office white-color workers often need communication between their managers, supervisors, and themselves. Office communication extends from the way that a user experiences a service. An effective office communication can bring these benefits; Providing positive influence on decision making by presenting a strong point of view and developing mutual understanding, delivering efficient decisions and solutions by providing accurate , timely and relevant information, enabling mutually benefit solutions, building health relationships by encouraging trust and understanding between the high level, middle level and low level staffs.

Effective office communication needs to clearly communicate its nature and purpose. Good communication ensures that all service staffs are sending out the same messages. Communication is also important for ensuring the service understands what users requires and why he/she talks about understanding users' needs and communication receiver can have effective communication skill to understand what he/she needs the another to do and the another knows he/she ought how to work by his/her task demand. Then, it will shorten much time. If the office has 100 staffs need to often communicate. However, if the office has good space management arrangement to let every staff can communicate easily and walks to anywhere to find the right staff to communicate conveniently. Then, they can spend less time to waste on communication issue. Then, their productive efficiency will be also influence to raise.

● Health and safe work environment influences productivity

Is a health and safe work environment can raise employees' work productive efficiencies indirectly? How and why it can influence employees' productive performance? Some occupations' working environments are easier to occur occupational accidents and diseases risks when the workers are working in the high health and safe risk's working environment. Hence, health and safety issues at these high life risk workplaces can be considered as a key to influence employees' overall performance. The idea that health and safety management program have positive impacts on productivity.

When one worker needs to work in this high risk of health and safe workplace. He/she will consider whether how his/her work behavior will bring suffer serious injuries for shorter or longer time from work related causes in possible. So, he/she will work carefully in order to avoid injuries occurrence chance. It is possible to influence whose work performance, low productive efficiency in order to avoid any occupational accident occurrences in the dangerous workplace.

If the employee feels danger when he/she needs to stay in the warehouses stable location to work often. Then his/her absenteeism day number will have increase, due to he/she feels that workplace accidents and occupational illnesses and can lead to permanent occupational disability, when he/she needs to attend the stable dangerous workplace to work in the warehouse. Hence, he/she will choose to apply holiday often in order to avoid injuries chance increasing when he/she needs to stay in the stable workplace location in the warehouse. It explains why companies increase need qualified, motivated and efficient workers who are able willing to contribute activity to technical and organizational innovations. So, healthy workers working in healthy working conditions are thus an important precondition for organization to work smoothly and productively. Hence, a health and safety workplace environment can bring these benefits to organizations as below:

It can prevent among workers of learning work, due to health problems caused by their working conditions, the protection of workers in their employment from risks resulting from factors adverse to health. The placing and maintenance of the worker in an occupational, environment adapted to his/her physiological and psychological, capabilities, mental , physical and social conditions of workplace and adequacy of health and safety measures are needed to any employees in order to bring positive impact not only on safety and health performance, but also productivity. However, identifying and quantifying these effects will difficult to be measured as well as the quality of a working environment has a strong influence on productive efficiency.

For one aviation air plane manufacturing factory, where workplace can environment will have high risk to occur occupational related accidents to cause employees' injuries. Hence, employees will be consider themselves safety when they need to work in high accident occurrence workplace. The bad consequence will influence such as absenteeism day number increases, leaving this kind of aviation air plane job of employees number increases, low productive efficiencies, due to there are many proficient experienced employees who choose leave this kind of high accident risk occupation. Consequently, any high accident occurrence risk workplace environment , employers need have good safe and health strategy to let their employees have confidence to work in this kind of high risk accident occurrence workplace if they expect low productive efficiencies effect is caused by high accident occurrence risk workplace factor.

● Employee personal
empowerment factor influences
performance

Is empowerment one good method to raise employee himself/herself effort in order to improve productive efficiency in organizations. Empowerment often consists of support groups, e.g. management's effective leading or trainer's training, course educational opportunities. Employee self-management education may impact to improve himself/herself job performance, e.g. increased self-empowerment, self-management skills and job treatment satisfaction.

Only organization's empowerment strategy can lead every employee to through improvements in the employee individual decision making efficacy, improvement task performance behavior by reviewing whether what are the employee himself/herself errors when he/she encounters any job difficulties, after he/she reviewed his/her task error and his/her manager feels his/her performance can be improved. Then, it can enhance satisfaction with the employee and his/her manage relationship and better access and raising efficient performance in possible . Hence, empowerment can let every employee to discover whether what task related difficulties he/she faces or encounters every day. When his/her manager give ideas to let him/her to know how he/she ought review his/her task error in a supportive education working environment, it aims to let the low performance or low inefficient employees to increase confidence to continue work in the organization. So, the employee turnover number will decrease , if the inefficient employees can feel that they can attempt to solve their task-related difficulties successfully by themselves. So, empowerment can increase social support, leadership and advocacy development , it has resulted in greater employee individual performance psychological empowerment, autonomy and authority to let every employee to feel to achieve to improve themselves efficiencies more effectively in any organizations.

For hospital organizational efficiency measurement empowerment influence case, how empowerment can influence hospital's efficiency raising? Efficiency is one of the most important indicators of hospital performance evaluation. Why do some hospitals' efficiencies poor? It is possible that mis management of resources, lacking health plan packages, e.g. coverage of basic health insurance, poor quality of care service, more payment demand for out-of pocket payment , quality of primary healthcare , healthcare providers neglect to concern potentially about service efficiency issues.

In fact, low hospital efficiency is the major problem to influence patients number to choose the hospital's medical service, e.g. when the hospital often needs patients to queue to wait for doctor's care medical service. They need to wait on hour at least or more when the hospital has many patients are waiting for its medical service. Then, it will influence them to choose another hospital to replace it , if the hospital 's medical fee is cheaper and it does not need patients to spend long time to queue to wait its medical service. So, service efficiency is important to influence patients consumers' positive or negative feeling to choose the hospital's medical service. Even, the hospital's doctors are famous or they own many medical working experience, if patients often need long time to queue to wait its medical service . Then, it will cause its patients number to be reduced .

These are variable factors to influence the hospital's inefficiency. They may include old speed hospital information system and medical record documents based on inefficient input and output variables. Input variables may include the number of hospital admissions, the number of nurses and the number of available beds. The output variable may include average of length of stay and bed turnover interval inefficient paper document record in the patient record administrative department.

However, to evaluate the hospital efficiency indicators may include technical, scale and managerial efficiency the out-based data development analysis approach and the variable returns to scales assumption was used. Based on the out-input based approach (maximizing the factors of medical service production), to increase efficiency the organization should be increased outputs.

Hence, when the hospital has good efficient evaluation method to measure every staff's performance , e.g. ward administrative clerk, patient registration clerk etc. Then, it can base on an put-put based approach and assuming a variable return to scale, there is capacity to improve technical efficiency and managerial efficiency in these any hospital different administrative units without an increase in costs and use of same amount of resources in relation to technical efficiency and managerial efficiency and scale efficiency of hospital's administrative labour individual task.

In conclusion, factors, such as modification of managerial practices, use of modern technologies tailored to the cultural, political and formulation of clinical guidelines to standardize the medical processes in order to reduce medical errors and increase the empowerment of health care buyers (insurance organizations), length of stay, management hospitals by specialist managers, administrative requirement, full time hospital physicians, limiting the authority of decision makers in relation to the recruitment of staff in accordance with the needs of the hospital and optimal allocation of beds, conducting economic evaluations and the type of hospitals ownership had an impact on the hospital efficiency significantly. By increasing the number of beds the hospitals efficiency decreases. Otherwise, optimizing the bed size can increase hospital efficiency.

However, the important factor to raise hospital overall staffs efficiencies empowerment is needed to let every hospital staff to review whether why and how himself/herself error is caused and he/she needs to review his/her errors to avoid to be caused from any negligence again in order to avoid patients' complaints again or reduce the patients' complaint number aims. So, empowerment of staff himself/herself error review factor is one major raising efficient good method.

II

Organizational environment factor influences the new employees production efficiencies

In psychological view ,in any organization's environments, they depend on the types of social and physical environment factors to influence employee personal behavior how to be caused. How and why does the employee select to do whose behavior? If the organization's physical and social environment is better, then it may influence its employees select to work hard. It is possible to bring productive efficient raising consequence.

In fact, when one new employee enters the new organization to work, he/she needs to learn how to adapt to cooperate with the organization's old employees to work together. So, it explains how and why organization's physical and social environment can influence the new employee individual motivation of behavior to work. In regarding new employee individual behavior by new employer's culture expectations as well as new employees. need to adapt of actions that are likely to productive positive outcomes and generally discard those that bring unrewarding or puniishing outcomes by new employer's treatment.

However, anticipated material and organization environment co-operation outcomes between the new employee and the organization old employees' cooperation, which are not the only kind of incentives that influence the new employee behavior of the new employee actions were performed only on behalf of anticipated external rewards and punishment from the new employer. In actuality, the new employee concerns considerable self-direction in the face of the new employer's organization's old employees competing influences. However, when the new employee has adopted an intension and an action plan. When, he/she works in the new organization for a period, he/she can't simply not back and visit for the appropriate performances to appear.

The new employee's new job goal will be motivated by enlisting self-evaluative engagement in activities rather than directly. By making self-evaluation conditional on matching personal new job standards, the new employee will give direction to his/her new job pursuits and create self-inventions to sustain his/her efforts for new job goal attainment. The new employee will select to do new task behavior to give him/her self-satisfaction and a sense of pride and self worth for the new job chance.

Efficacy beliefs also play a key role in shaping the new employees' behavior to do their tasks by influencing the types of new organization's activities and working environments, the new employees choose to set into any factor that influences the employee's choice behavior can affect the direction of employee personal career development in the new organization. This is because the organizational working environment influences operating in the employee how to select working environments continue to work. Thus, by choosing and shaping the new organization's working environments, new employee can have a hand in what they expect.

In conclusion , when a new employee chooses the new organization to work. He/she must need to adapt the organization's new working environment. If he/she feels difficult to adapt or accept to the organization's new working environment, then he/she will be influenced to work inefficient or poor productive performance , due to he/she feels unhappy to work the new organization's working environment and the new organization's manager will dissatisfy his/her performance and complain or give verbal warning to dismiss him/her. Then, it will bring the poor consequence to let the organization's inefficient productive performance effect. If many new employees feel difficult to adapt to work in the new organization. Then, inefficient productive performance will be influenced to keep a long term.

So, it implies that the organization will need to change its organizational culture in order to let many new employees can adapt and accept this new organizational culture to work happily if the organization expects new employees work to raise productive efficiency successfully.

● Raising efficient and effective
interview psychological methods
In human resource department, interviewing and selecting the most right applicants to do different kinds of positions, it is one part of HRM function. If the interviewer need to spend more time to interview to decide whom is the most right applicant to do the position in one day, e.g. 50 at least , even more applicants number as well as he/she can also make the more accurate personal selection decision to choose the most right applicant to do the position after the interview day. Then, the interviewing process needs to be avoided to spend more time to choose the most suitable applicant to do the position within the day. It is difficult to judge whether whom ought be the most right applicant to do the position, if there are more than 50 applicants , they are needed to be interview in the day. The consequence will bring HR department can spend extra time to do the interview task, but it can have enough staffs and time and resource to do other urgent or important task at the interview day. It will bring this question: How to apply psychological method to raise interviewer's efficiency to shorten to spend extra time to do interviewing tasks ? I shall explain some psychological methods to attempt to let interviewers have more confidence to select the most right applicant in short time as below:
1. Behavioral interview skill
The interviewer can apply the actual behavioral interview method to let the interviewee to answer how he/she deals the matters, he/she feels that it is the best decision in order to judge and analyze whether whom applicant is the most suitable to be selected, e.g. describing the situation, he/she needs or the task that he/she needs to accomplish. The situation may be from a previous job, any relevant event, describing the action he/she took and be sure to keep the focus on him/her , e.g. discussing a group project or effort in the team; explaining what results he/she achieved, what happen? How did the event and what dis the applicant accomplishes? What did the applicant learn?
In the behavioral-based interview. the interviewer can need the applicant to attempt to explain examples clearly in order to judge whose analytical skill

whether he/she is the suitable applicant to do the position. The interviewer may ask the applicant to identify some examples from whose post experience where he/she demonstrated top behaviors and skills that employers typically seek. To judge whether his/her examples should be totally positive, such as accomplishments or meeting goals, the other half should be situations that started at negatively , but either ended positively or he/she made the best of the outcome.

This behavioral interview test aims to review whether the applicant's every example answer, he/she can provide an appropriate description of how he/she demonstrated the desired behaviors. In the behavioral interview, the interviewer can attempt to judge whether the applicant has good imagine effort to mind any relatively small set of examples to respond to a number of different behavioral questions to satisfy the right example are applied to the right situations in the limited interview time. Hence, behavioral interview can let the interviewer to make more accurate analysis to judge whether whom applicant(s) has (have) good analytical effort to solve any work-related situational problems in the most reasonable way or attitude in order to select whom is the most right applicant to do the position.

2. E-mail interviewing in qualitative research

E-mail interviewing is another good interview method to select right applicant to do the managerial level position. E-mail interviewing can be in many cases a viable alternative to face-to-face telephone interviewing. Internet-based qualitative research methods may include online personal interview and virtual focus groups. However, it brings two questions: What opportunities and challenges does online in depth interviewing present for collectively qualitative data? How can in depth e-mail interviews be conducted effectively?

The applicant targets may be the top-level manager, advertising executive , sales manager, human resource manager etc. management position applicants. They need to answer any complex or difficult interviewing question by email in the limited time, e.g. how to solve one case study problem , how to give recommendation to solve the situation problem. The interview participants may be recruited by tool/method of psychological test questions, the interview questions may be interview guide in a single e-mail and follow yp, length of email data collection period may be up to 10 weeks, the number of e-mail or follow up exchanges may be several number. The electronic formal and require little editing or formation before the applicants are processed for analysis all e-mail interviewing questions.

So, they need to answer any managerial case study problem in limited time. It is one good managerial interview test method to evaluate whether whom applicant has the best analysis effort in order to the managerial position, because they need to find the best solutions to give recommendations to attempt to solve any situational problems in any un predictive case study problems. For example, when the applicant or a focus group of discussion applicants whom need to spend the maximum half hours to give recommendations to discuss to solve one complex or difficult case study problem either between the interviewer and the another interviewee applicant or between the group of five to ten interviewees (job applicants) themselves. Thus, after the interviewer sent the one case study question to let the applicants to know by every email channel. The interviewer needs to judger whether whom one applicant or one of the focus group applicants their recommendations are the most reasonable to solve the case study managerial situational problem within half hour to one hour. Then, the interviewer can make more accurate judgement to select whether whom has the best analytical effort to do the managerial position.

3. The effectiveness of motivational interviewing for young or older adult applicants selection process

How can apply case management skills to be effective to prepare any interview motivation? How to do the most effective and efficient to meet the objectives of the interview? Some interview techniques used may vary the based on the individuals involved in the interview. For an interview with the young age applicant more require a different approach than an interview with a senior adult applicant. The following are one pointers to assist with preparing for the interview as below:

Knowing the purpose of the interview and what needs to be accomplished . What is the expected outcome? Gathering all forms that need to be completed or signed having the interview and making list of questions that need to be asked, knowing the key facts and topics to be discussed, during the interview. Gathering factual information that may be helpful. Opening mind is needed in the whole interview process. Making an appointment for the interview and arranging sufficient time to set fully participate in the interview. Taking notes during the interview, let the participants know in general terms the reason notes are being made and how they will be used, opening ended questions invite the applicant to provide more information usually begin with other words who, what, where, how, asking one question at a time and keeping wording simple and specific, defining any terms that may be unfamiliar to the applicant , giving the interviewing participants in the interview an opportunity to ask their one questions or to clarify anything that was discussed, closing the interview with a review of the information discussed and facts gathered, reviewing any follow-up that is to be done by the case manager or others involved in the interview.

In an efficient and effective interview, the interviewer needs have good body and spoken word communication to the interviewee or the position applicant. Because a good communication can reduce waste time or avoid the extended longer interview time if the interviewer can make good communication to impact good message to let the applicant to understand what is the mean to his/her interview question. What he/she wants to know, the total impact of a message includes ,e.g. 7 % verbal (words), 38% vocal /volume, pitch, rhythm etc. and 55% body movements (mostly facial expression). The interviewer's body and verbal behavior can make more clear message to let the interviewee(job applicant) to understand what answers are he/she wants to know mostly. Hence, an efficient and effective interview can let the interviewer to control and manage the whole interview to evaluate whether whom the applicants' answers or feedbacks are more reasonable to be acceptable to be better to compare other applicants to apply the position more accurately.

III

Interview psychology methods

- What are common psychology methods of recruitment choice?

Can any psychology methods are used to choose who will be the best recruitment applicant(s) in any recruitment stage more accurate? Can the interviewer observe the applicant's psychological phenomenon to judge whether the applicant can be the best or the most suitable applicant in the recruitment stage more accurate? To answer above these questions. We need to know why a systematic scientific procedure is an essential component to achieve any psychological method(s) to test candidate individual ability to judge whether who is the best or the most suitable applicant to do any position in any organization.

A psychologist can follow a systematic scientific procedure which has theoretical base in order to explain and interpret the psychological phenomenon of the applicant to decide whether who is the best or the most suitable applicant to do the position in the organization.

On the one hand, in order to obtain the applicant's psychological response from individual applicant, there are a number of psychological tools or instruments are used during the interview process. The responses are taken on these tools constitute the basic data which are analyzed to study the applicant experiences, e.g. working experiences, life experiences, mental processes and behaviors. On the other hand, in order to understand every applicant's behavior during the interview process. The different psychological methods can be applied for solving different applicant's individual behavior (individual mental problems) to judge who will be the best or the most suitable applicant to the position in any organization. Because different situations will cause the applicant to choose how to do or perform different behaviors to persuade the interviewer believes who is the best or the most suitable applicant to do the position in the organization. Thus, whose performances will be shaped by many factors both intrinsic and extrinsic to him or her in any interview process.

The common psychological methods of interview process include such as: For observation psychological method example, when shopping in the market , the researcher must have noticed various activities of the consumers . When he/she observes the consumers their activities, the researcher also think about as to why who are doing those activities and probably the researcher reaches a conclusion about the causes of such activities. So, observation is as a psychological method of enquiry is often understand as a systematic registering of events without any deliberate attempt to interface with variables operating in the event which is being studies.

Thus, observation psychological method seems to be applied to judge who is the best or the most suitable applicant to do any position in any organization in any interview process. Such as in any interview process, the interviewer (observer) can use this method to judge or observe every applicant's face and behavioral performance to feel whether who is the best or the most suitable applicant who own ability or confidence or qualification or experience to already to do the job to achieve the recruitment result is more accurate. For example, the interviewer (observer) can attempt to give one simple or difficult task to test whether whom the applicant has the more effort of the induced stress on task performance in the short time observation test in the on part stage of the interview process.

However, observation is also divided into either participant or non-participant both types, depending on the role of observer (interviewer). In the case of interview participant observation, the interviewer mixes up with the job (task) performance event test under study and conducts concerns the interview test, e.g. group discussion interview test, the applicants and the interviewer will discuss one or more than one topic(s) which concern(s) on relating the position requirement issue. So, the interviewer can analyze whom applicant(s) can talk the most reasonable evidences to support whose opinions to argue the topic against the other applicants together among of them in the short time group discussion, e.g. between 15 minutes to 30 minutes. It aims to let the interviewer can have enough time to record whose opinions to analyze whose opinions are the most reasonable argument to support whose main points to win this position among these interview competitors in the short time group discussion.

Thus, the interviewer needs to participate the group discussion to ask every applicant any questions and let them to attempt to solve any challenges in the whole group discussion. After the group discussion, then the interviewer can have more effort or confidence to judge whom applicant (s) is/are the most suitable or the best applicant (s) to do the job for his/her organization more accurate.

Otherwise, as in the case of interview non-participant observation, the interviewer maintains an optimum distance and has little impact on the interview event. Such as the interview group discussion test. The interviewer won't ask any questions to let the applicants to attempt to answer. Otherwise, he/she will let the applicants have chance to ask any questions or answer the questions among of their discussion related to the topic. So the interviewer's role is a listener, who only needs to listen every applicant how who can ask and can answer any questions to decide who can talk the most correct or the right or the most reasonable answers to answer their questions in the short time group discussion. Then, the interviewer can record all applicants' questions and answers to make the judgement to decide who will be the right or the most suitable applicant to do the position in her/him organization more accurate.

● Why does need to test the applicant's psychological behavior in the interview process?

To answer this question, we need to know why any large or middle size organizations which need have human resource department. To challenge of today's HR managers is to create a pool of good employees in the organization. It starts from selection process of the employees. So, interview has been used as an important selection method by HR managers for long time. The cost of rehiring the importance of hiring the right person for right position first. It requires a reliable and valid interview process. Although, any interview won't guarantee 100 percent success in hiring the best employees into any organization, but the proper application is at least, will improve the chances of hiring the best applicant for the job the organization. The importance is given to the selection of right employees for the right positions. Firms are now realizing the value of the good employees because who can make a difference through their job performance. So, various selection methods are now being used to identify the right candidate.

" Interview" has emerged as a very useful tool in this regard. It is a very common selection method and has a high predictive validity for job performance (Robertson, & Smith , 2001). The main purpose of the interview is to select the right candidate for the right job. The importance of conducting an effective interview is also rising. So consensus was found among the HR experts regarding the effective interview techniques. There are a number of existing literatures regarding the techniques of an effective interview, but every few literatures exist regarding a systematic approach of conducting exist regarding a systematic approach of conducting an effective interview.

This is a very few literatures exist regarding a complete interview process that shows a clear path to the employers for selecting right employees. A lot of interview technique are available, but the problem arises regarding the use of these techniques in a concrete manner. A systematic approach of interview will facilitate the tasks of HR managers in selecting the right applicant for the right position.

(Stevens, 1997) author indicated the whole process of the interview has been described in terms of "3D"- Development, discussion and decision. This study is particularly important for three reasons. First , it will help the HR mangers to think about the employee selection interview in a concrete manner. Second, it will help them to use a number of interview techniques in an effective way that will ultimately increase the chance of hiring the right person for the right position. Third, it will enrich the existing literature of selection interview.

(Stevens, 1997) author also explained that the growing importance of good employees will cause a challenge to the HR managers. The selection process of today's HR manager is becoming complex and challenging. Undoubtedly, the overall aim, of the selection process is to identify the candidates who are suitable for the vacancy or wider requirement of the HR plan. " Interview" has been used as a ' critical selection method ' by HR managers. The interview is the most valid method in determining an applicant's organizational fit, level of motivation and inter-personal selects.

Whetton & Cameron (2002) cited steps of process of conducting an interview, what they named as People-oriented selection interview process. Here is explains the interview process: P=prepare, E=establish rapport, O=obtain information, P=provide information, C= lead top close and E= evaluate.

So, it seems that the candidates' behavior individual performance in the interview process can be predicted whether who is(are) the most suitable or the best to do the position in the organization from the interviewer's observation. So, it also means the candidate's attitude in the interview process can perform to let the interviewer to feel whether who is suitable or the best to do the position in the organization . Thus, observation of the applicant individual performance, it is an interviewer's best interest to find good prospects, hire them and have them stay in the organization.

Therefore, the interviewees are needed to be provided sufficient information about the job and organization to have enough time to prepare before who will go to interview fairly. It aims to let every candidate has enough confidence to prepare to answer any questions in further interview process fairly. So, the development stage is a good preparation for the interview facilitates the effective interview process. To aim to let the candidate have enough preparation to interview , it should begin long before the first question is ever asked fairly.

In conclude, HR department seems an essential department to any middle or large organizations nowadays. It does not attribute only recruitment function to any organization, it also attribute the chance to give one psychological test function to evaluate whom applicant has the more experience and qualification and effort to do any position in any organization. If the interviewer has not prepared any psychological method to test any applicants to judge whether who has the more effort to do the position. Then, I believe the interview result will be more failure and more inaccurate to employ the most suitable applicant , due to who lacks the enough effort and qualification and experience to perform to finish any tasks or duties of the position . So, it is important why any organization needs have good psychological method to test and observe the applicant's psychological behavior in the interview process?

● Occupation psychological
test methods
How to apply psychological recruitment
strategies effect/manage in the
recruitment process?

HR (human resource) managers understand accept that poor recruitment decisions continue to affect organizational performance and limit goal achievement. In this case, many jurisdictions to identify and implement new effective hiring strategies will be serious issue to any HR departments to concern.

Acquiring and retaining high-quality talent is critical to any organization's success. So, recruiters need to be more elective in their choice. Since poor recruiting decisions can produce long term negative effects, among their high training and development costs to minimize the incidence of poor performance and high turnover to impact staff morale, the production of high quality goods and services. Thus, HR managers must seek all possible methods for improve their output and provide the satisfaction to their clients require and deserve. The provision of high quality goods and services begins with the recruitment process.

(Schuler, Randalls, 1989) explained recruitment is as " the set of activities and processes used to legally obtain a sufficient number of qualified applicants at the right place and time. So that the applicants and the organization can select each other in their own best short and long term interests.

Thus, it seems that successful recruitment begins with proper employment planning and forecasting. So any one organization needs analyze what kinds of positions of future needs talent available within and outside of the organization and the current and anticipated resources that can be expected to attract and retain such talent. Thus, HR manager needs have one successful strategy to be prepared to employ in order to identify and select the best candidates for its developing pool of human resources.

In common, one successful recruuitment strategy involves these several processes of :

Step one : Development of a policy on recruitment and giving life to the policy.

Step two: Needing assessment to determine the current and future human resource requirement of the organization.

Step three: If the activity is to be effective , the HR requirements for each job category and functional division /unit of the organization must be assessed, identification within and outside the organization of the potential human resources pool.

Step four: Job analysis and job evaluation to identify the individual aspects of each jobs and calculate its relative worth, assessment of qualifications profiles, job descriptions that identify responsibilities and requirement skills, abilities , knowledge and experience, determination to pay salaries and benefits within a defined period.

Step five: identification and documentation of the actual process of recruitment and selection to ensure equity and laws.

Thus, the psychological recruitment strategy for the interviewer includes how to ask interview questions, how to give interview scores and panellists' comments, results of tests (where administered). Because and length of interview time for the interview. There are any interview main contents to any interviewer needs to concern how to arrange interview process.

For example, nowadays, it is popular internet recruiting. Although, interviewer can reduce time to arrange and spend time to interview any applicants, due to the interviewer can interview any applicants from whose organization website . Specially, there are many similar potential interview competitors to apply to the position at the same time. Otherwise, internet recruiting is not all positive. Such as some applicants skill place great value in face-to-face interactions in the hiring process. Such applicant's are likely to ignore jobs posted, impersonally on time.

I shall indicate these sample recruitment strategy to explain how to influence every applicant's choice to apply the job or not apply the job as below:

The first is online recruiting. This online recruitment strategy has a large percentage of employees are hired by human service agencies for every level jobs are seeking their first career job. The newspaper want ads are not an effective recruitment source for most of today's applicants. Placing vacancy announcements online is more effective and economical than using most traditional forms of advertising. However, online recruitment is designed to close this gap: Not reaching majority of applicants, especially young graduates.

The second is campus recruiting and job fairs. This campus recruiting strategy attracts both professional and paraprofessional applicants, who can be effectively recruited at job fairs sponsored by state workforce development agencies. However, college recruiting can be a very effective method for attracting applicants for professional jobs. The possible psychological advantages to applicants that includes any employers will send team of HR representatives to any colleges to provide an opportunity for job seekers to ask both job specific and hiring process/benefits questions; sending an ambassador to classrooms to quest lecture; schedule experienced employees or supervisors to ask on a hot topic in the human or service field at a local college or university. However, this campus recruiting strategy has a large percentage of employees hired, but need to improve overall applicant.

The third is university partner developing a variety of recruitment strategy. University partnership benefits include to collaborate with university deans and professors to help student interest in the field as well as to develop program partially covering college tuition and other expenses of college students who agree to work for the human service agency for specified periods of time. Its recruitment strategy aims to develop a variety of recruitment strategies with area universities, community colleges and schools of social work to encourage students to pursue careers in the human services. It's weakness lacks enough applicants with specialized social work degrees.

The fourth recruitment strategy is target recruitment. Employers may used a more diverse workforce that better reflects the client population who serve. For example, employers may need to recruit employees with specific language skills or with specialized degrees , e.g. criminal juice. It' weakness lacks of diversity in targeted jobs.

The fifth recruitment strategy is internships. Interns sometimes are paid stipend, but in most instances interns are fulfilling an academic requirement of the college or university. Although supervisors and/or cause work staff must spend time supervising and training interns, the potential payoff is having a known applicant who is familiar with agency operations. Its weakness is needed to improve overall applicant pool.

The sixth recruitment strategy is maintain a pre-screened applicant pool. It has a pool of pre-screened, interviewed applicants always available to be called for a second interview with the hiring supervisor. When, using this approach, it's important to minimize the amount of time between the initial interview and the second interview to prevent top quality applicants from being hired human resources will need to do continuous recruiting and screening , even when there are no current vacancies. It's weaknesses include that some
human services organizations delay hiring until staff vacancies reach crisis proportions. They than initiate a recruitment process that is designed to bring new employees on board as soon as possible . The unfortunate result is hiring employees who meet the minimum requirements, but nothing more. It also has too many applicants get hired with only the minimum credentials.

The seventh recruitment strategy is realistic job previews. Realistic job previews are designed to prevent applicants from taking jobs that who have life knowledge of or are not suited to perform. It is a recruiting tool is designed to reduce early turnover by communicating both the desirable and the undesirable aspects of a jobs before applicants accept a job offer. It can be in the form of videos, oral presentations, job shadowing opportunities. It's weakness includes unwanted turnover among new workers who did not understand their job when who were hired.

The final recruitment strategy is improved hiring flexibilities in highly centralized systems. It means many public-sector human service agencies are regulated by merit systems that make it different to attract and maintain the interest of top-qualify applicants. Top applicants in today's economy are searching the interest for jobs that are available now. They aren't interested in taking a civil service exam and sitting on eligibility lists for months. In some systems requirements and lengthy inflexible scoring processes wash out well qualified applicants. It's weaknesses include hiring process takes too long, high qualify applicants are looking elsewhere for jobs.

● How to apply occupational psychological
test method to test applicant's ability?

Occupational psychological interview method is the application of the science of psychology to test applicant individual work ability. For example, any interviews can apply occupational psychologists' test method to attempt to test applicant individual performance, motivation and wellbeing of the organization in the workplace. If any interviewers can attempt to apply occupational psychologist test method to test any applicant individual working abilities in interview. It brings this question: How can the interviewer develop, apply and evaluate a range of tools and interventions to test the applicant individual working abilities across many different areas of the workplace?

The occupational psychological test method can include these psychological skills to test every applicant individual ability in interview. Such as : Psychological assessment means selecting and assessing the applicant individual ability using interview enquiring method, e.g. in interview, enquiring applicant concerns on how to solve crisis deal issues when challenges cause in any workplace, assessments of what the applicant's main ability centers are. Situational judgement tests, e.g. how to solve challenges in different situations and personality questionnaires and cognitive ability tests. Profiling jobs are matching requirements to the applicant's future performance. Developing and choosing is valid, reliable, fair and suitable selectin procedures.

Thus, the psychological enquiring questions can concern on work motivation, performance, appraisal and management, leadership power influence and negotiation, employee engagement and commitment, citizenship and positive behaviors or counterproductive in workplace, psychology of group teams and teamwork different aspects, which have similar points , such as concern organizational behavior questions. It aims to test the applicant how to deal any immediate crisis in the organization if the interviewer decides to employ him/her.

The key focus of how to achieve one effective psychological test to the applicant in the interview. It focuses on key areas , such as the applicant personal goal attainment, interview performance, the applicant's mind on innovation and creativity aspects, and well being in the workplace how the applicant explains who will perform supposes who did the job in the workplace.

In the interview, the interviewer needs the applicant to explain to let him/her to understand how the applicant's relation and motivation in the organization. The interviewer also needs to know how the applicant can solve any challenges in workplace in the situation test interview. Because conflict resolution is a challenging environment to work in. However, any downsides are offset by the rewards of being able to help protect both the organization and its employees from the psychological , physiological and economic costs of conflict. Because conflict will occur in possible in any workplaces. Thus, the interviewer ought to ask the question to let him/her to know the applicant will solve if who did this position.

Human factors is a discipline concerned with how the successful interview applicant (future employee) works effectively and safely. It considers a employee's environmental , organizational, job and individual characteristics. These factors will affect the organizational successful interview applicant (future employee) behavior and it is past of the interviewer's job to analyze these and to give recommendations for change to improve human performance to the organization if who selected to employ these applicants in every time interview. Thus it seems occupational psychological test method can give benefits to the interviewer to understand more to the applicants to judge whether who will be the most suitable applicant(s)to do any positions in whose organization more accurate decision in any interviews.

● Selecting and evaluating
assessment methods

● How selection assessment methods are applied to choose the best applicants ?

Organizations compete in the war for talent. So, one effective selection assessment method can help any organizations to choose the best applicant(s). Using scientifically proven assessments to make selection decisions, even though such assessments have been shown to result in significant productivity increases, cost savings, decrease other critical organizational outcomes. I shall indicate common misconceptions about selection tests, such as: Screening applicants for conscientiousness will yield better performers , then screening applicants for intelligence, screening applicants for their values will yield better performers , then screening applicants for intelligence, integrity tests are not useful because job candidates misrepresent themselves on these types of tests, unstructured interviews with candidates provide better information than structured assessment processes and using selection tests creates legal problems for organizations rather than helps to solve them.

There are numerous different types of formal assessments that organizations can use to select employees. The first step in developing or selecting an assessment method for a given situation is to understand what the job requires employees to do and what knowledge, skills and abilities individuals must posses in order to perform the job effectively. This is typically accomplished by conducting a job analysis . For job oriented job analysis recruitment example, providing test by stating fact and answer questions, gathering and reviewing information to obtain evidence or develop background information on subjects, integrating diverse information to uncover relationships between individuals, events or evidences.

Other assessment methods focus on how measuring the best applicant who are required to perform job tasks effectively, such as various mental abilities, physical abilities or personality traits, depending on the job's requirements. If one were to assess whether candidates could solve decisive and communicate effectively. Alternatively, if one were selecting an administrative assistant, such as the ability to perform work conscientiously with speed and accuracy would be such more important for identifying capable candidates. Some worker-oriented or job analysis data are used as a basis for developing assessment method, that focus on a job candidate's underlying abilities to perform important work task.

In general, any organization interviews only divide either internal or external both selection. Internal selection refers to situations where organization is hiring or promoting from within, whereas, external selection refers to situations where an organization is hiring from the outside. When some assessment methods are used more commonly for external selection. (e.g. cognitive ability tests, personality tests, integrity tests). There are numerous examples of organizations that have used one or more of the following tools for internal selection, external selection or both. I shall explain what the differences for these interview test methods as follow:

What is cognitive ability tests. These assessment measure a variety of mental abilities, such as verbal and mathematical ability, reasoning ability and reading comprehension. Cognitive ability tests have been shown to be extremely useful predictors of job performance and thus are used frequently in making selection decisions for many different types of jobs (Hunter, J. 1986, Ree, M.J. & Teachout, M.S. 1984, Gottredson, L.S. 1982).

Cognitive ability tests typically consist of multiple choice items that are administered via a paper-and-pencil instructment or computer. Some cognitive ability tests contain test items that need various abilities, e.g. verbal ability, number ability etc. But then sum up the correct answers to all of the items to obtain a single total score. The total score then represents a measure of general mental ability. If a separate score is computed for each of the specific types of abilities, then the resulting scores represent measures of the specific mental abilities.

Job knowledge tests mean these assessments measure critical knowledge areas that are needed to perform a job effectively. Typically, the knowledge areas measured represent technical knowledge. Job knowledge tests are used in situations m where candidates must clearly possess a body of knowledge prior to job entry. Job knowledge tests are not appropriate to use in situations where candidates will be trained after selection on the on knowledge areas who need to have. Like cognitive ability tests, job knowledge tests typically consist of multiple-choice items administered via a paper-and-pencil instrument or a computer , although essay items are sometimes included in job knowledge tests (Hunter, J. 1986).

Personality tests that assess traits relevant to job performance have been shown to be effective predictors of subsequent job performance. The personality factors that are assessed most frequently in work situations include conscientiousness, extraversion, agreeableness, openness to experience and emotional stability (Barrick, M.R. & Mount, M.K. 1991, Costa, P.T. Jr., & Mccae, r. R. 1982).

Research has shown that conscientiousness is the most useful predictor of performance across many different jobs. Although some of the other personal factors have been shown to be useful predictors of performance in specific types of jobs (Hough, L.M. 1992). It can consist of several multiple choice or true/false items measuring each personality factor. Like cognitive ability and knowledge tests, which are also administered in a paper-and-pencil or computer format.

Biographical data (biodata) inventories, which ask job candidates questions covering their background, personal characteristics or interests have been shown to be effective predictors of job performance (Stokes, G.S. & Owens, W.A. 1994, Shoenfeldt, L.F. 1999). Another form of a biodata inventory is an instrument called an " accomplishment stored". With this types of assessment, candidates prepare a written account of their most meritorious accomplishments in key skill and ability areas that are required for a job , e.g. planning and organizing, customer service, conflict resolution (Hough, L.M. 1984).

Integrity tests measure attitudes and experiences that are related to an individual honesty, trustworthiness and dependability (Sackett, P.R. & Wanek, J.E. 1996). It is typically multiple-choice in format and administered via a paper-and-pencil instrument or a computer.

Physical fitness tests are used in some selection situations. These tests require candidates to perform general physical activities to assess one's overall fitness, strength or other physical capabilities necessary to perform the job.

Situational judgement tests provide job candidates with situations that who would encounter on the job and viable options for handling the presented situations (Mecichmann, D., Schmitt, N. & Harvey, V.S. 2001). depending on how the test is designed , candidates are asked to select the most effective or most and least effective ways of handling the situation from the response options provided. Situational judgement tests are more complicated to develop than many of the other types of assessments. It is because more difficulty in developing scenarios with several likely response options that are all viable, but in fact, some are reliably rated as being more effective than others. Situational judgement tests are typically administered in written or paper-and-pencil test booklet or on a computer.

Assessment centers are a type of work sample test that is typically focused on assessing higher-level managerial and supervisory competencies (Thornton, G.C III 1992). Assessment centers usually last at least a day and up to several days. They typically include role-play exercises in -basket exercises, analytical exercises and group discussion exercises. Trained assessors observe the performance of candidates during the assessment process and evaluate them on standardized rating. Some assessment centers also include other types of assessment methods, such as cognitive ability, job knowledge and personality tests. It should be noted selection purposes that assessment centers aren't only used for comprehensive development feedback to participants.

Physical ability tests are used regularly to select workers for physically demanding jobs, such as police officers and firefighters. These test are similar to work sample tests in that who typically require candidates to perform a series of actual job tasks to determine whether or not who can perform the physical requirements of a jobs. Physical ability tests are often scored in a pass/fail basis. To pass, the complete set of take that comprise the test must be properly completed within a specified timeframe.

How to criteria for selecting and evaluating assessment methods in interview?

Properly identifying and implementing formed assessment methods to select employees is one of the more complex areas for HR department to learn about and understand. This is because understanding selection testing requires knowledge of statistics, measurement issues and legal issues relevant to testing.

I recommend any interviewers need to understand important criteria to decide to choose which kind of interview test is the suitable to test applicant individual abilities in every interview such as below:

The first criteria includes validity. Validity means the extent to which the assessment method is useful for predicting subsequent job performance. Adverse impact means the extent to which protected group members , e.g. minorities, females and individuals over 40 score lower on the assessment than majority group members.

The second criteria includes cost. Cost is both to develop and to administer the assessment. Applicant reactions means the extent to which applicants react positively versus negatively to the assessment method. For example, cognitive ability test. on the positive side, this type of assessment is high on validity and low on costs. However, it is also high on adverse impact, moderately favorable. Thus, when cognitive tests are inexpensive and very useful for predicting subsequent job performance, score significantly lower on them than whites. There is no simple, formulaic approach for selecting " one best" assessment method, because all of them have advantages and disadvantages.

However, the most important consideration in evaluating on assessment method is its validity. Validity refers to whether or not the assessment method provides useful information about how effectively an employee will actually perform once who is hired for a job. Validity is the most important factor in considerate whether or not to use an assessment method because identify who will doesn't accurately identify who will perform effectively on a job has no value to the organization.

There are two major forms of validity: criterion-related validity and content validity is a simple example will illustrate how criterion-related validity can be established. Assume that a sales job requires employees to have a high level of customer service orientation and an organization decides to implement a selection test that assesses prospective applicants on their customer service skills. In order to show that the client skills assessment is a valid predictor of performance , it must be shown that individuals who score higher on the assessment perform better. On the job and individuals who score lower on the assessment perform less well on the job. Thus, validity in this case would be defined as a meaningful relationship between how well people performed on the assessment and how well who subsequently performed on the job. Content validity approach to validation involves demonstrating that an assessment provides a direct measure of how well candidates will actually perform to job. This type of validation requires analyzing the job to identify the tasks that are performed.

What are the differences between criterion related versus content validation. Criterion-related validity can be used to evaluate the validity of any assessment where individuals receive scores that reflect how well who perform on the test and these scores are subsequently shown to relate to how well who perform on the job. Content validation can only be used to validate assessments that provide a direct measure of how well candidates perform job tasks or the content of the jobs, such as work sample tests. Otherwise, criterion-related validity evidence or validity . Thus, it is more desirable to obtain if it is possible to conduct a successful unbiased performance measures must be available. Unfortunately, performance appraisal ratings, which are the most commonly used performance measures can be inaccurate and often fail.

Adverse impact is examined by comparing the proportion of majority group who are selected from a job to the protected group members who are selected. When organizations are and should be interested in selecting the higher quality work force possible, many are also concerned about selecting a diverse workforce ought not using measures that will systematically produce adverse impact against protected groups.

In conclusion, either if an assessment method is shown to produce adverse impact and the organization wished to continue the last of that assessment, there are legal requirements to ensure that the method must have demonstrated validity or if an organization uses an assessment that produces adverse impact that produces adverse impact without the validity evidence. The organization will encounter challenges against which it won't be able to prevail. When evidence of validity can be used to justify and defend the use of measures that produce an adverse impact many organizations nonetheless attempt to apply the adverse impact produced be their assessment methods to extent possible in order to minimize potential interview wrong recruitment decisions and lack of diversity concerns issues to recruit any the most suitable applicants to do any positions in any organizations.

Reference

Barrick, M. R. & Mount , M.K. (1991). The big five personality dimensions and job performance: A meta-analysis, personnel psychology, 91, 1-26.

Costa, P.T. & Jr., & McCrae, R.R. (1992). Four ways five factors are basic. Personality and individual differences, 13, 653-665.

Gottredson, L.S. (Ed). (1982). The g factor in employment, Journal of vacational behavior, 29(3).

Hough, L.. (1992) The big five personality variables construct confusion: Description versus prediction human performance, 5, 135-155.

Hough, L.M. (1984). Development and evaluation of the " accomplishment record" methods of selecting and promoting professonals. Journal of applied psychology, 69, 135-146.

Hunter, J. (1986). Cognitive ability, cognitive aptitudes, job knowledge and job performance, Journal of vacational behavior, 29, 340-362.

Meichmann, D., Schmitt, N., & Harvey, V.S. (20010. Incremental validity of situatinal judgement tests , Journal of applied psychology, 86, 410-417.

Ree, M.J. Earles, J.A., & Teachout, M.S. (1994), Predicting job performance: Hot much more than g. Journal of applied psychology, 79, 518-524.

Robserton, I. T., & Smith, M. (2001). Personnel Selection. Journal Of Occupational And Organizational Psychological Psychology, 74(4), 441-472.

Sackett, P.R. & Wanek, J.E. (1996). New developments in the use of measures of honesty, integrity, conscientiousness, dependability, trustworthiness and reliability for personnel selection, personnel psychology, 49, 787-829.

Schuler, Randalls, S: Personnel and human resources management. Third edition, 1987.

Shoenfeldt, L.F. (1999). From dustbowl empiricism to rational constructs in biodata. Human resource management review, 9, 147-167.

Steven, Kay Cynthia (1997). Effects of pre-interview beliefs on applicant's reactions to campus interviews. Academy of management journal, 40(4), 947-966.

Stokes, G.S. Mumford, M.D. & owen, W.A. (Eds.) (1994). Biodata handbook paloacto, CA: CPP Books.

Thornton, G.C. III (1992). Assessment centers in human resources management Addison-Wesley,

Whetton, D.A. & Cameron, K.S. (2002). Developing Management , Skill 5th edition, reading, MA: Addison Wesley Longman.

IV

Employee satisfaction measurement

How to measure employee satisfaction ?

It has close relationship between employee satisfaction and work motivation. The right staff can work in the right position which can affect the effective productivity of the company. Also, if employees feel satisfactory , then the company can have more chance to raise (increase) productivity, responsiveness, quality and good customer service performance. However, if any company want employees to work efficiently, then which needs to know that one of the biggest internal strength of the organization is the relationship and communication between employees and the managers. Besides, the biggest improvement is also needed in the field of the financial rewards, because most of the employees are not showing high satisfaction to them.

Whether how to measure what the level of employee satisfaction is accepted to achieve the stable productivities? The main subjects will be leadership and motivation to answer this question. For example, supermarket organization, whether which factors could be improved in the target work in supermarket organization every day? I shall assume it has perhaps to cause job dissatisfaction if the supermarket has only the power of money as motivator in supermarket organization. Any organization has its culture. As supermarket organization has also itself culture. However, I believe that cultural traits that can affect the employee satisfaction in any supermarket organizations. Although, any supermarket organization has usually different departments to cooperate work together. Hence, if it has good organizational culture to make different departments, e.g. store, food, wine, stationery, clerical, counter etc. departments staff who can have good communication to work in comfortable cultural supermarket environment together, then its staff can have more ability to achieve the best work performance. How to solve this department cultural difference of challenge, I suggest any supermarket needs have good HRM plan to control its department's employee behaviors.

Human resource means the staff who work in a organization and the contribution who make with whose skill, knowledge and competence. The most important successful factor of knowledge based economy in which intelligent organizations are the key aspects of economic growth in the global economy. Why does organization need to satisfy employee needs? Because any staff trend to change working places often, any staff can change their workplaces to gain more respect and to feel more valued in their jobs. So, it can avoid staff turnover (leaving) whose organization very easy if the employer can satisfy whose staff needs. Thus, human resource plan is needed to achieve policies, recruiting and selecting work force, training and development, workplace planning, ensuring fair treatment of employees, ensuring equal opportunities, assessing the performance of employees, managing employee welfare, providing a counseling service for employees, managing the payment and rewards systems, supervising health and safety procedures, disciplining individuals, dealing with dismissal or promotion, negotiation, ensuring the legality of organizations etc. concerning about managing employees' positive psychological issues, in order to build positive emotion to them.

● How can leaders satisfy employee needs?

Any organization needs have good leaders because leaders act to provide satisfaction or more likely to offer means of satisfaction to whose team members. Leaders don't necessarily motivate. A successful leader understands the needs of the others and persuades them to act in a certain way. A good leaders can make whose workers see that following the views of the leader's workers will get the most satisfaction out of their work. However, a person can be motivated without leadership. But leadership, however, can't succeed without the motivation of the follower's side. If a staff has the feeling that who can perform a higher level job, himself/herself who have the motivation to attend courses or train in another way to be able to perform at the required higher levels.

Douglas Mc Gregor's famous classification of theory x versus theory y is applicable for leadership approaches. In general, any staff has two kinds of psychological characteristics of either theory x person or theory y person. Theory x assumes that in general most staff find working distasteful and usually avoid doing it if it is possible . That is why most staff must be controlled and directed, even threatened to perform the way the organizational goals will be reached. Theory x also assumes that staff want to be controlled and directed rather than take responsibility and that staff lack ambition. Otherwise, theory y on the other hand, is more likely to have roots in the recent knowledge of human behavior. It assumes that physical and mental effort in work is as natural as play or rest. So, leaders need to judge whether whole managing staffs (team members) who belong to theory x or theory y kind of staff. Then, who will have more accurate method to lead whose team members easily.

What level of satisfaction to the organization's staff can achieve the best performance. I feel that when the organization can reach the willingness level to be told the extent to which any one of staff has motivation and commitment or self-confidence to accomplish a certain task. So, the willing level is the most satisfactory maturity level to achieve the best performance psychological factor to any organization. Because of the maturity satisfactory level of employees is high, the employees are both willing and able to do the tasks given more efficient. Otherwise, if the maturity satisfactory level is moderate, leaders can concentrate on the relationship and participate in the decision making and willing processes as workers are able but may be unwilling to complete their tasks. Only a little bit of encouraging is needed. Otherwise, if the mature satisfactory level is low, workers are willing but may be unable to complete the tasks, so leaders must push to sell the tasks and let the workers do the rest or leaders must tell workers what to do.

In this supermarket organization case, if supermarket's grocery department and logistic department and clerical or cashier departments and fishing/meet etc. department whose employees' maturity satisfactory level is low, then it is possible that who are unable and unwilling to complete whose individual department daily tasks efficiently and these different department managers need to concentrate on both relationship and task aspects to raise whose maturity satisfactory level to be moderate level, even the high level in order to achieve the best performance.

Leaders also need to concern staff job satisfaction issue. Job satisfaction is the reflection of a good treatment. It also can be considered as an indicator of emotion well being or psychological health, even job satisfaction can lead to behavior by an employee that affects organizational functioning. Furthermore, job satisfaction can be a reflection of organizational functioning. Why can job satisfaction influence any organizational performance? The reason is some people like to work and who find working is an important part of their lives. Some people on the other hand find work unpleasant and work only because who have to do support their lives. However, job satisfaction tells how much people like their job. Job satisfaction is the most studied field of organizational behavior. It is important to know the level of satisfaction at work for many reasons and the results of the job satisfaction studies. In the workers' point of view, it is obvious that feel respected and satisfied at work, it could be a reflection of a good treatment. In the organization's point of view good job satisfaction can lead to better performance of the workers which affects how the result of the organization to achieve its productivities for long term.

So, any employer or leader can not neglect whose staff what job satisfaction level to whose staff in any time. In general, if whose staff can not feel job satisfaction, who will choose to leave whose current employer more easily.

● How does one company raise employee
efficiency

What makes one company more successful than another? It is possible to concern better products, services, strategies, technologies or perhaps a better cost structure. However, the final source is the best staff performance of good productive factor, because it can cause these result, also employees who are engaged significantly outperform work group and who are tangible asset to raise the company's competitive advantage where employees are the differentiator, engaged employees are the ultimate goal. What factors can affect job satisfaction. I find that agency theory might be helpful to explain how organizations need to think of their human resource responsible in producing the output needed by organizations to meet shareholders value. Agency theory is concerned with issues related to the ownership of the firm when that ownership is separated from the day-to-day running of the organization. It assumes that in all but owner managed organizations, the owner or owners (known is agency theory as the "principle" of an organization must best authority to an agent -corporate management to act on their behalf) Shenkel, R. Gardner, C. (2004, pp. 57-59).

The principle recognizes the risk, here and act on the assumption that any agent will look to serve its own as well as the principle interests as it fulfills it contract with that principal. However, this is not the situation in real life situation. As all agents are perceived to be opportunistic. Agency theory is therefore used to analysis this conflict in interest between the principal (shareholders of organizations) and their agents (leaders of these organizations). The agents in keeping with the interest of the shareholders and organizational goals turn to use financial motivational aspects like bonuses, higher payrolls, pensions, sick allowances, risk payments to reward and retained their staff and enhance their performance. However, given this perception, the principal in an organization will feel unable to predict an agent's behavior in any given situation and so brings into play various measures to do with incentives in other to tie employee's needs to those of their organization. However, the fundamental problem, dealt with is that drives or induces people to exploit their potential resources in the way they do in organization. The issue of motivation and performance are who positively related. By focusing on the financial aspect of motivation problem likes bonus system, allowances perks, salaries etc. I believe financial motivation and trying to Mallow's Basic needs non financial aspect why comes in when financial motivation has failed. So, employers need to evaluate the methods of performance motivation in whose organization in organizing some motivational factors like satisfies and dissatisfies will be used to evaluate how employees motivation is enhanced other, than financial aspects of motivation. I believe that with the changing nature of the work force, recent trends in development, information and technology, the issue of financial motivation becomes consent on one of the most important assets in an organization. The potential role of money is as conditioned reinforce and an incentive which is capable of satisfying needs and an anxiety reducer and serves to erase feelings of dissatisfaction.

In general, any organization can use performance or efficiency to measure its productivities. Such as, performance means the act of performing; of doing something successfully; using knowledge as distinguished from merely possessing it; a performance comprises an event in which generally one group of staff (the performer or performers) behave in a particular way for another group its staff.

Efficiency means the ratio of the output to the input of any system. Economic efficiency is a general term for the value assigned to a situation by some measure designed to capture the amount of waste or friction or other under desirable and undesirable economic feature present. It can also be looked as a short run criterion of effectiveness that refers to the ability of the organization to produce outputs with minimum use of inputs.

Why does employer need to know how to motivate whose staff? What is meaning of motivation? Motivation means as the psychological process that give behavior purpose and direction to behave in a purposive manner to achieve specific unmet needs, an unsatisfied need, and they will to achieve respectively. So, salary, job satisfaction, job goal , reward will be task -related motivation since goals direct staffs' thoughts and action. So, motivation to staff needs have these factors expected. For example, phychological needs are the bottom of the staff, such as foods, air, water and shelter. Any staff needs a salary that enable then to afford adequate living conditions. Then, staffs need safety, psychological needs. They need to work for a secure working environment free from any threats or harms and organizations can provide these need by providing employees, with safety working equipment e.g. hardhars, health insurance plans, fire protection etc. Next, staffs need social needs and the needed to be loved and accepted by other people. Esteem includes the need for self-respect and approval of others. Finally, self actualisation is the top psychological need, it is capable of being to develop the staff himself/herself full potential. The rationale holds to the point that self actualised employees respect valuable assets to the organization human resource.

Why do employers need to concern flexible working arrangement? Employers need to concern flexible working arrangement if who hope employees can raise productivities and efficiencies to achieve the best work performance. Flexible working describes any types of working arrangement that gives some degree of flexibility on how long, where and when employees work. Because employees need time to learn a familiar phase with workplaces, flexible working arrangements have been an option in many employment sectors for a long time, helping employment meets the changing needs of their customers and staff. The reasons include customers expect to have products and services available outside of the traditional 9 to 5 working hours; employees want to achieve a better balance of between work and home life and organizations want to meet their customers and employees needs in a way that enables them to be as productive as possible. Organizations need to produce any products and services of the right quality and at the right price, under constant pressure. To meet customers' demands, sometimes new ways of working have to be found to make the best use of staff and resources. Flexible patterns of work can help to solve those pressures by maximising the available labor and improving customer service.

At employers, organizations also have a duty of care to protect whose staff from risks to their health and safety, e.g. stress caused by working long hours or feeling pressure to need to balance work and home life. However, flexible working can help to improve the health and wellbeing of employees and by extension, reduce absenteeism, increase productivity, and enhance employee engagement and loyalty. Flexible working time includes per time works often used in hotels, restaurants, warehouses etc. flex time. Mostly used in office based environments for staff below managerial level in public and private sector service organizations; annualized hours often used in manufacturing and agriculture where there can be big variations in demand throughout the year.

Thus, I feel the flexible working and work life balance benefits can include a more efficient and productive organization, a more motivated workforce, better retention of valuable employees, a wider pool of applicants can be attracted for vacancies, reduced levels of absence and increased customer loyalty and working hours that the best suit the organization, its employees and its customers applications of knowledge about how people as indicators and groups, act within the total organization, analyzing the external environment's effect on the organization and its human resources, missions, objectives and strategies. So, it concerns how to predict staff psychological feeling to learn how to motivate who to work efficiently.

Why does manager need to concern employee's individual diversity need? Also, manager needs to know each person is substantially different from all others in terms of their personalities, needs, demographic factors and past experiences and/or because who are placed in different physical settings, time periods or social surroundings. This diversity needs to be recognized and viewed as a valuable asset to organizations. Selective perceptions may lead be mis- interprectation of single event work or create a barrier in the search for new experience. Managers need to recognize the perceptual differences aiming the employees and manage them accordingly. These whole person effects between the work life and life outside work and management focus should be in developing not only a better employee but also better person in terms of growth If the whole person can be developed, then benefits will beyond the firm into the larger society in which each employee lives. Because individual's behavior are guided by their needs and the consequences that results from their acts. In case of needs, people are motivated not by what others think who ought to have but by what who themselves went. However, motivation of employee is essential to the operation of organizations and the biggest challenge faced by managers. Organizations ought give more opportunities to let employees who can contribute their talents and ideas because many employees actively seek opportunities at work to become relevant decisions the stay or leave the organization, also managers ought concern any employee's individual skills and abilities and to be provided with opportunities to develop themselves.

V

Organizational behavior theory

● What is system approach?

What is system approach? All parts of an organization interact in a complex relationship. Systems approach takes an across, the board view of people in organizations and analyses issues in terms of total situations and as many factor as possible that may effect people's behavior. Three theoretical frameworks, the cognitive behavioristic and social learning frameworks, the basis of any organizational behavior model. The cognitive approach is based on the staff and organization expectancy, demand and incentive concepts. Because staff behavior on the basis of the connection between stimulus and response in any organization. The social learning approach incorporates the concepts and principle of both the cognitive and behavioristic frameworks. In this approach, staff behavior is explained as a continuous interaction between cognitive is explained as a continuous environmental determinants. In the organizational behavioral model, there are some dependent variables like productivity, absenteeism turnover, job satisfaction, deviance absenteeism, turnover, organizational citizenship behavior etc. The reason of which staff try to understand. The cause of these outcomes like with some variables of individual, groups and individual level, these variables are called independent variables.

It seems different organizational workplace environments will influence staff's different variable causes to decide how to do whole daily behaviors, how to fit to work in the organization. So, any manager needs to know what every staff is individual characteristics to judge how to manager himself/ herself. For example, if the staff is theory x person, who will dislikes work and will avoid it if possible, who lacks responsibility, has little ambition and seeks security above all who must be controlled, threatened with punishment to get who to work. So, the manager's attitude is needed to control whom. Otherwise, if the staff is theory y person, who will feel work is as natural as play as rest. People are not inherently lazy, who have become the way is as a result committed, the staff has potential, under proper condition who learn to accept and seek responsibility, who has imagination creativity that can be applied to work, so manager who is to develop the potential to the staff and help who release that potential toward common objectives.

Any organization depends on the external environment for two kinds of into outputs, which it transforms into outputs and then releases in the hope that external environment will accept them. First, human input, employees and natural resources. Second, non human inputs, e.g. equipment, information, raw materials. However, organization needs to adjust to environmental demands, e.g. customer complaints, market research, financial reports, in order to keep to improve performance easily.

How to raise organizational efficiency? As systems theory indicates organizational effectiveness and time is considered as one element of a larger system of number of elements. The organization takes resources (inputs) from the external environment, processes these resources and returns them in changed form (output). According to system theory, effectiveness criteria must reflect the entire input process, output cycle, not simply output and must also reflect the interrelationships between the organization and its outside environment. In relation to environmental circumstances organization passes through different phases of lifecycle like forming, developing , maturing and declining and the appropriate criteria of effectiveness must reflect the stage of the organization's life cycle.

The criteria of effectiveness are also time based short run (results of actions concluded in a year or less), intermediate run (when effectiveness of individual, group or organization is considered for a longer period, perhaps five years and long run for this the time frame is indefinite future. The four short run effectiveness criteria are quality, productivity, efficiency and satisfaction. Three intermediate criteria are quality, adaptiveness, efficiency and satisfaction. The two long run criteria are quality and survival. So, any organization needs have effectiveness criteria because effectiveness criteria can reflect the stage is of the organization's life-cycle (which includes stages of growth, maturation and decline) and short, intermediate and long term perspectives. Quality means the total quality control rank among the most used programs to meet customers' changing demand. Hence, employee's individual satisfaction will influence productivity. Because productivity reflects the relationship between the organization's inputs and outputs and measures of productivity include profit, sales, market share. For example, patients released, clients served concerns the relationship between employees' satisfaction and clients' overall satisfaction. When the employee feel more satisfactory, then who will work more efficient or who will serve the clients more pleasant. Then, the customers will have more chance to feel more satisfactory from the staff's individual service.

Efficiency is the ratio of outputs to inputs. It focuses on the entire input process output cycle, emphasis in out and progress. Measures of efficiency include rate of return on capital, or assets, unit cost, waste, downtime, occupancy rates and cost per patient/student etc. customers. Satisfaction meets employee needs. It recognizes the organization is as social system that benefit its participants. Measures of satisfaction include turnover, absenteeism and employee attitudes. Adoptive means the degree to which the organization can and does respond to internal and external changes. It relates to management's ability to sense environmental changes and changes within the organization. There are no specific measure of adaptiveness, but certain progress, e.g. employee training and career counseling increase its capacity to deal with it. Finally, development means the ability of the organization to increase its capacity to deal with environmental demand. So, if the organization hope to be survival in the long term, then it needs to achieve training programs and organizational development to be represent the organization's investment in survival.

● How can satisfy to employees' needs ?

How can satisfy to employees? Because a high rate of employee is directly related to a lower turnover rate. Thus, keeping employees' satisfied with their careers should be a major priority for every employers. Reasons why employees can become discourages with jobs and design, including high stress, lack of communication within the organization, lack of recognition, or limited opportunity for growth. So, management need actively seek to improve these factors to avoid if who hope to lower turnover rate. However, some employee will often be feel bored with the work because there is no intrinsic motivation to succeed. Finding the daily same job duties can reduce the individual's motivation to succeed to raise desire to show up to work and to do the job well. In this case, the employee may continue to come to work, but whose efforts will be minimal.

Stress is another factor to cause low performance. Branham (2005) indicates that " it seems clear that one quarter to one half of all workers are feeling some level of dysfunction, sue to stress, which is undoubtedly have a negative improve on their productivity and the probability that they will stay with their employers."
However, stress can be caused by these factors, e.g. in the situation, when a company can't or won't supply the tools necessary to produce or work efficiently on the job. This produced higher stress levels because these workers are expected to perform at certain rates, yet who are unable to do so. This results in lower productivity and higher turnover because quotes can't be met by the employees. On staff knowing that management is able to provide the tools essential for the position is important to employee trusting the intentions of their employer.

Dissatisfaction with the job many come from sources other than stress or poor fit between employee and the job. Employers that are deemed unethical by workers because who appear to care about company revenues, rather than the employees that are working for them. In the result, the employer may lead to job dissatisfaction, and raise the company's turnover rate.

Lack of communication in the workforce is another major contributor to dissatisfaction. Bad communication leaves employees feeling disconnected from the organizations. This is detrimental to wellbeing of the company because when an employee feels neglected, who will trend to perform at a lower level because who feels unsure of whose position within the company and wonders what whose purpose is within the workplace. Also, employees may be unaware of how whose performance measures up to that of their co-workers and have no sense of who can improve. So, without communication, it becomes difficult for employees to make any progress in their efficiency. The employee may feel uncomfortable in the workplace, of who feel rarely be praises for the quality of whose performance. Finally, those factors cause the failure to provide employees with opportunities to grow within the company results in employee frustration to cause whose poor performance and low productivity.

Whether can bonuses increase raise employee satisfaction and team performance? In some occupations, I feel bonuses can raise staff performance, such as bonuses lead to happier and it can be used in the form of donations to charity organization or bonuses in the form of expenditures to pharmaceutical sales teams and sport teams organizations. However, employees are becoming more and more unhappy, more and more of time at work, hardly a formula for a healthy and productive workplace. In this increasingly negative environment, how can employers incentivize their employees to increase their happiness, job satisfaction, and job performance? Certainly, designing effective incentive schemes is a central challenge for a wide range of organizations form multi-national corporations to academic departments. Identifying the most effective strategies, a variety of incentive schemes and are suggested such as bonuses from fixed salaries to pay-performance from commission to end-of-year bonuses. It is based to assume that the best way to motivate employees is to reward them with money that who then spend on themselves. In general, existing methods of increasing workplace performance, including individual-based and team based bonuses schemes, which trend to reveal both benefits and unexpected cost. Whether the benefits of improving social life in the work phase can increase employee citizenship behaviors to satisfy the organization actual needs from these bonuses compensation schemes.

What is the effect of money on employee's job satisfaction and performance? On one hand, monetary bonuses have been found to have positive effects, increased productivity effort, performance and job satisfaction. Individual bonuses increase job satisfaction in part. On the other hand, individual incentives, such as large bonuses are often surprising ineffective increasingly employee morale and productivity. In an effort to prevent such negative competitive dynamic that can result from individual based-bonuses, organizations often change to incentivize employees for their collective performance, encouraging cooperation and teamwork rather than competition. Otherwise, in some cases, team based compensation schemes have been shown to raise this sense of cooperation between team members, inducing them to exert additional effort toward helping another worker to work together linked to employee morale and performance.

Whether bonuses can have a causal impact on employee. In fact, individual incentives, such as large bonuses are often surprisingly ineffective in increasingly employee morale and productivity. Also, rewarding individual employees can produce negative outcomes, as employees become reluctant to share information with others even at the expense of reduced output. In an effort to prevent such negative competitive dynamics that can result from individual based bonuses. Importantly, such increased cooperation due to interdependent rewards has been shown to improve team performance, suggesting that team based bonuses may be an effective means of improving employee social life. As with individual based bonuses, however team based bonuses offer important advantages, but also potential drawbacks. I suggest that prosocial bonuses can have a causal impact on employee satisfaction and performance, such that providing employees with money to spend on themselves.

How effective organizational communication can affect employee attitude, happiness and job satisfaction. Communication has been studied with regard to performance and job satisfaction, but the relationship with employee attitude and happiness has not been done in a higher education setting. The value of communication in an employee's choice to be happy is explained as it affects the individual, team and overall organizational culture. Attitude and happiness have been recognized by communication examination of organizational culture and emotion in the workplace. For example, for frontline employees are needed have cheerful and positive in the face or any situation. So, it requires the owners, managers and supervisors communicate to whose team efficiently.

Communication with telecommuting or remote workers is a consideration that organizations must take seriously more than 24 million people were working remotely in 2008 year (World at work, 2009) and that number is steadily rising. Teleworkers report feelings of isolation, uncertainty, a lack of trust and lower organizational commitment with lower job satisfaction. Managers may not communicate the save way with remote workers as who do with employees who are in the workplace each day. Improve communication is important to hold employee engagement initiatives together, particularly in government public sector organizations must communicate throughout the entire cycle of planning, conducting and acting on engagement. So, I suggest some effective communication method to raise productivity and improve performance. Such as ensuring that employees understand their work expectation between their jobs and the organization's mission, meeting regularly with staff members, providing feedback as performance , as well as opportunities to grow and developing , even fail as a way to learn and holding employees accountable for performance, including with poor performance.

How to make a difference at work be more meaningful and purposeful workplaces. The workplace provides a wealth of opportunities and possibilities through which anyone can make a difference every day. Whether it's one person, one team or one organization, everyone has the capacity to create positive and meaningful change in their workplace in both small and large ways. How to foster the work motivation of individuals and team? Nowadays, some evidence supports claims that motivational programs can increase the quality and quantity of performance from 20 to 40 percent. Moreover, motivation can solve three types of performance challenges: first, staff are refusing to change often, second, allowing themselves to be distracted and not persist at a key task and/or third, treating a task as familiar, making mistakes but not investing mental effort and taking responsibility because of overconfidence.

Imagine that more than 50% of staff in your organization decided that from this point, who would work one extra day a work without an extra day of rest. What impact would their decision have on your organization's bottom line? What is the value of a 50% increase in performance by 100% of the workforce? Assuming that you may know some of the 50% , who do the minimum and a few of the 80% who could work much harder, do you think that there is anything that would convince people to work harder than who are now? Is it possible that half of your staff who admit that who could work much harder might actually decide to increase whose performance by 20% or more if they were adequately motivated? The best evidence suggests that highly significant performance increases are possible when motivational strategies are implemented (Clark & Estes, 2002).

● How to achieve work motivation strategy ?

Work motivation is the process that initiates and maintains goal-directed performance. Without motivation , even the most capable person will refuse to work hard. Thus, motivational performance gaps exist whenever staff avoid starting something new, resist doing something familiar, stop doing something important or attention to a less valued task, or refuse to work smart on a new challenges, instead use old familiar, but inadequate solutions to solve a new problem (Clark, 1998).

How can we make sense of such variety and get benefits as performance technologies? Is any given situation where we want to increase work motivation, we must determine what will convince staff to start doing something new or different increase their persistence at an important task and investment mental effort. The staff must believe that the motivator driving their enhanced performance will directly or indirectly contribute significantly to what who need to feel successful and effective. The motivator's work has to cost less than the value of the increased performance and it must meet both ethical and legal requirement. When it might appear that solutions have to be tailored to the different demands of individuals in a team. In the absence of a clear vision leading to work defined business and performance goals, people substitute their own goals and whose goals may not support the organization. So, it is important to ask about evidence for the benefit of all work rules and what might be cost of the rules more eliminated. What is gained by rules that staff can't take or eat in certain areas? Why can't they decorate their work space in ways that suit them? How much of staff's behavior must you control to achieve business goals? One way to motivate and staff and simplify organizational work processes is to eliminate all unnecessary rules, policies and procedures.

To learn how to motivate staff, we need to learn how to predict staff's individual psychological behavior. Organizational behavior is a scientific discipline in which large number of research studies and conceptual developments are constantly adding to its knowledge base. It is also an applied science, in that information about effective practices in one organization is being extended to many others. Organizational behavior is the systematic study of human behavior, attitudes and performance within an organizational setting, drawing on theory methods and principles from such disciplines as psychology, sociology and cultural anthropology to learn about individual perceptions, values, learning, capacities and actions when workings in groups .

Nowadays, why employees hope employers can give them to enjoy well life balance. The reasons may include care commitments to children or elderly relatives, education commitment that limit availability at times of the week/month/year, duties and/or interests outside of work, needing to be available for people making a greater sense of well being and reduced stress levels. How to arrange flexible working in organization? For example, an employer may be thinking about introducing annual hours in order to increase production levels to meet infrequent rises in demand because who can work well where, there are peaks in works, the workforce is required to be available with little notice. The employer could decide to meet these increases in demand by introducing overtime because it provides flexibility to meet fluctuations and it could be a smaller change to the organization than annual hour. However, there are many different forms of flexible working. Flexible working can cover the way working hours are organised during the day, week or year. It can also describe the place of work, such as homeworking or the kind of contract, such as a temporary contract. Anyway, flex time can operate in different ways depending on business need. On the one hand, there may be a system to allow employee to build up additional hours, which can be used to leave early, come in late, or take longer periods off with early, come in late, to take longer periods off, with approval from line management. An example of this might be an assembly line or call center where staffing must be scheduled to meet customer demand. For example, an employer needs to extend the hours that whose business is open to 8 AM to 8 PM, but can't afford the extra overtime. how to manage flex time approach could help provide the additional hours, reduce staff numbers at quiet times and minimize the need for overtime. Employer may benefit from the opportunity to travel outside of peak hours and/or accommodate personal responsibilities, such as the school runs part time work is the must common types of flexible working. It's potential benefits include customer demands on be met and machinery can be caused more efficiently if part time workers cover lunch breaks/evening shifts and weekends, the working day can be arranges around caring responsibilities and/or other commitments, employees can continue to work increasing whose own leisure time. But part time work also have potential challenges, such as increase in training, increase in administrative and recruitment costs, e.g. recruiting two part timers could longer than one full times and providing a continuous level of service may be difficult.

Overtime is normally hours that are worked over the usual full time hours. It can be compulsory or voluntary . A recognized system of paid overtime is more common with hourly paid staff than salaried staff. Potential benefits include that employer can provide flexibility to meet fluctuations in demand, short term labor shortage without having to recruit extra staff overtime. Even with premium payments, is often less costly than recruiting and training extra staff or buying extra equipment. However, overtime work has also potential challenges, include when working excessive overtime can affect an employee is performance health and home life. It can result in higher absence levels and unsafe working practices.

Job sharing is a form of part time working where two or more people share the responsibility for a full time job. They share the pay and benefits in proportion to the hours each works. They share the pay and benefits in proportion to the hours each works. Job shares may work split days, split weeks or alternate weeks. it's potential benefits include that if one job sharer is absent, due to illness or holiday, the other can carry on with at least half the work, who can help meet people demand , e.g. both shares being present when workloads are heavy, a wider range of available, who can help people with caring responsibilities and/or other commitments to continue working. It is potential challenges also include extra induction, training and administration cost, replacement may be difficult if one job sharer leaves, added responsibility on supervisors/managers, who must allocate well fairly and ensure that the job shares communicate effectiveness. If the shared role involves managing on supervising staff can find it is difficult working for two managers.

Shift work is a pattern of work in which one employee replace another doing the same job within a 24 hour periods. Shift workers normally work in crews, which are groups of workers who make up a separate shift team. it's potential benefits include it can reduce costs by using equipment more intensively and taking advantage of cheaper off peak. It's potential challenges include it can increase wage and labor costs, it can disrupt employees' social and domestic lives, it can upset employees' body and affect an employee's performance and health.

Employers ought concern employee engagement issue. Different professions have their own specific, which need to be addressed during the engagement building process. For example, for hospital workers, safety issue is of a high importance as who deal with different kinds of sicknesses, whereas for teachers or the issue of stress and emotional exhaustion many be of more importance.

To learn how to satisfy employees, content with their work experience, was a good formula for success, as a satisfied employees, who wanted to stay with a company, contributed to the workforce stability and productivity. However, satisfied employees may just meet the work demands, but this won't lead to higher performance. In order to compete effectively, employers need to go beyond satisfaction. Therefore, modern organizations expect their employees to be full of enthusiasm to work. Other researchers state that employee engagements is the best fool in the company's efforts to gain on competitive advantages and stay competition. Though, the notion of engagement is relatively new, and it is already a hot managerial topic and it is rare to find an HR or managerial related that doesn't mention employee engagement. These researchers agree that engagement creates the prospect for employees to attach closely with their managers, co-workers and organization in general and engaging environment is the environment when employees have positive attitude toward their job and are willing to do high quality job.

It seems that how to develop good engagement workplace environment can influence employees' satisfaction, then it can influence whose performance or productivity. So, they have close relationship. however, it is even harder to build engagement within the specific group of employees in the situation, when the knowledge about the specifics of their work-life is missing. Different occupations need have different engagement workplace environments and engagement methods to let employees to feel satisfaction. For example, engagement of administrative workers in the educational organizations is rarely studied and poorly understanding, even though these employees have a significant influence in the institution and the quality of their performance contributes to the quality of relationships with faculty students and the public. So, understanding the administrative personnel work life perception is important to educational organizations. How schools can implement engagement to achieve target to improve administration employees (administrative workers) whose performance, students, faculty public satisfaction and other organizational outcomes. Because whose performance is not save to factory workers to cause how many product quantities manufacturing per hour to calculate, whose need to use service quality to measure performance.

I feel it is better in the situation when organizations have a better understanding of the administrative personnel work-life perceptions, it is easier for them to create appropriate engagement building tools. Such as, administration employees working at small sized education organizations are more engaged, and this might be due to the reason that they have better relationships with colleagues and experience a greater sense of belonging than their collages from larger education organizations. Futhermore, Johnsrud and Rosser (1999) also suggest that the smaller the institution, the more positive administrative workers moral and consequentially the higher chances for their engagement. Therefore, result of this study can be applied only to the educational institutions of the similar size. Furthermore, results of this study can't be used for similar organization in order contributions.

What factors can influence the engagement of administration staff. I feel that significant variables factors include: working conditions, job fit, role fit, time spent interacting with students and length of employment on campus. As some researchers working conditions were found to be a significant and positive factor influencing engagement, this means that better working conditions increase the chance that the employee will shoe in higher level of engagement person job fit was defined by Edwards (1991, as referenced in Kristof, 1996, p.8) as " the fit between the abilities of a person and the demands of a job , i.e. demands-abilities or the desires of a person and the attributes of a job needs supplies". Job fit also focuses more on the formal aspects of the work, when role-fit includes both established and new tasks, which core out in teams, as team members' roles include formal tasks as well as informal socially defined tasks. The only factor , which was found to have a negative influence on the engagement of administrative workers was employment history, meaning that the higher level of employees were working within an educational organization, the lower level of engagement who showing.

I shall recommend to measure the engagement level of employees and to find out the specific engagement that need to be improved, the quantitative research with questionnaires as the main source collecting data was needed to choose to any educational organizations. Because questionnaires can produce number data, which is a quantitative approach. The educational administrative workers can be compared with each other within the category of engagement and can point out the factors driving engagement, which need to be improved. These numbers are the basis for further analysis and recommendations. The factors, which can be chosen for the investigation, include meaningful job autonomy at work, performance feedback, institution development opportunities, organizational support, procedural justice, social support from colleagues, supervisory support, social climate etc. The reasons to choose these factors to investigate because the meaningful job can increase psychological meaningfulness for the employee and therefore increases engagement. The above factor meaningful job has been included in the list. Besides, job characteristics can increase meaningfulness for the employee and are positively rarely to job engagement. However, educational administrative workers' moral has an influence on their perception an attitude to the job. The same study pointed out that the moral of administrative workers in educational organization is influenced by number of factors, such as working atmosphere, relations with colleagues and supervisors. For example, social support from colleagues and supervisory support is concerned to moral issue. Social climate factor is concerned to reward and recognition issue.

Why employers need to concern employee moral issue. For example, any clinic organization has complex interpersonal relationships within the clinical domain and the critical issues are faced by nurses on a daily basis, indicate that morale, job satisfaction and motivation are essential components in improving workplace efficiency, output and communication amongst staff. Drawing on educational , organizational and psychological research, that the ability to inspire morale, staff morale which is a fundamental indicator of sound leadership and managerial characteristics. These includes role preparation for managers, understanding internal and external motivation, how internal motivation to nursing staff and the importance of attitude when investing in relationships. Because this factors can influence nurse performance. As the field of nursing, amongst money others, the concepts of developing emotional self-awareness in staffs, self-control, adaptability in initiating in management, and organization teamwork in social networks have been poorly applied. Despite this, it has been suggested that nurse and physical collaboration is one of three strongest predictors of psychological empowerment of nurses (Larrabee et. 2003).

Relationships on the ward can influence to nurse satisfaction and personal professionals are closely linked to self-esteem or person's own morale. So, morale of nurse occupation can influence performance to serve patients. In health care industries, how to create healthy working clinical environments and encourage nursing staff for leadership and management roles, the issues of morale and motivation need to become primary concerns in the ward setting. Because any nurse service will fill with dread, fear and anxiety to whose patients if who neglects to concern care morale. So, nurses need to concern motivating behavior and discourages pessimistic feelings and performance. The reality is that some people naturally posses a high level of this internal motivation, these who focus on the internal feelings of satisfaction who will attain despite any difficulties who face along the way. Executives are coached, athletes are coached, why not health care professionals? The nature of helping others through clinical care provision may preclude staff from asking for help themselves.

Has it relationship between boosting morale and improving performance in the nursing occupation? For example, healthy working environment and system may be assisted through the regularity of coaching key staff, e.g. nurses in hospitals need to create any clinic ward organizations. Clinical will environments with good retention, work satisfaction and high quality measures. Nurses can also learn how to self-coach be more self aware and develop themselves. In the nursing occupation, linking nurses' daily work to long term ambitions will impose their motivation, boost their self-confidence and assist them to function at a higher performance level. Coaching will also help staff recognize their own management styles, and identify their leadership strengths and areas for improvement. Because nursing work is frequently rewarded by patients' gratitude. Nurses within clinical settings often comment on the patients' capacity to say thank you and their appreciation of how nurses contribute to their well being. So, the success of their health care service. In fact, performance appraisal is ideally about recognising the direction an individual nurse wishes to pursue concern how health care moral behavior to nurses to achieve to satisfy patient's individual need to reduce complaint occurrences to build healthy clinic environment to let nurses to work enjoyable.

Why absenteeism will influence performance? Unscheduled absenteeism is a popular problem for U.S. employers, conservatively costing $3,600 per hourly employee per year and $2,650 per salaries employee per year, the majority of employers have limited ability to accurately and regularly track how much absenteeism is reducing their bottom line earning, effective absence management systems can track absenteeism, manage absence policies and work schedules, and control overtime, allowing management to reduce lost earnings, also reducing absenteeism will also help employers better meet production and service demands without requiring an increase in headcount. Commonly, the un schedules absenteeism rate in the U.S. hourly workforce is approximately 9% almost one in ten workers is absent when who would be at work. There are considerable direct and indirect costs are increasing. Not only should managers be motivated to reduce absenteeism because of the excess costs, but without absence tracking tools, employers can't adequately estimate their accurate liabilities. However, absenteeism causing is probable due to poor health to the individual employee. So, who will perform poorly to influence whose productivity to be worse. Why is there such little focus on absenteeism, compared to other costs, health care or low productivity or poor service performance costs for example? So absenteeism can raise much different workforce related costs. The excess costs arise cause disruption to the business, make it difficult to deloy the workforce, and have a profound effect productivity, profit margins and poor employee morale.

However, improving employee health can at most, only reduce absenteeism by one-third, as two-thirds of absenteeism is caused with non-sickness (personal reasons, feeling of entitlement, family issues). In the result, the direct impact is reduced or poor delayed production or customers are not being served. How to solve absenteeism challenges? Generally, the employer was using a five day schedule, but demand was such that employees were asked to come in on the weekend on a regular basis. The employees disliked working, so many consecutive days with no time off, which led to very high absence rates. The shortages of employees results in demand not being met and customers were dissatisfied. The organization has to replace missing workers with other employees or contractors and pay overtime or higher rates. Overtime levels are 28% higher in facilities with low absenteeism. Excess staffing plan, such as headcount is higher than necessary in order to cover unplanned absences. For example, the employer routinely increased headcount by 13% on weekends to cope with extra absenteeism on a Saturday and Sunday. It is less usual for a salaried employee to be replaced when absent. Instead, the demands of customers (internal or external) are not met and depending on the employee's position in the company, the ability to create revenue may be affected. Excess absenteeism can also lead to increased health care cost, greater safety issues and accidents, high turnover, and poor morale or performance. To achieve significant reductions in the excess costs with absence, the manager must reduce the rate of absenteeism and the subsequent effect that absenteeism has no the business. The first step is accurately and efficiently tracking absenteeism rates and patterns on a regular basis. The majority of organizations don't have an automated means to track every instance of absence in one system and therefore lack the visibility necessary to address this business problem. Once the root causes of the problem are known. The manager can consider what steps need to be taken. There may include using rules engines and process automation to consistently enforce absence policies, compliance with union, state and rules, improving absence management technology and increasing employee satisfaction with the workplace, reducing overtime costs by selecting employee to cover for absence based on their competence, training and hours worked during the week, accurate reports of absenteeism , patterns over time and root causes.

In order to take full advantage of opportunities for business expansion and growth. Human assets investment strategy is very important to any organizations. For example, airport organization, it needs good employees serve to provide excellent customer services to satisfy the increase flight slots at airports. So good human assets investment strategy can drive focus on safety, innovation and globalization and create programs for motivating employees to enable them to fully demonstrate their abilities. Such as airport training is needed to be given by lecturers, include rank based and elective training to airport service industry. Methods are such as on site courses, supporting the career development to any airport different rank of staffs to promote on environment where individual employees can display their capabilities to the maximum possible extent in their respective roles. In special, giving women career training establishing a mentor system under which senior employees provide ongoing direction and support for junior and new employees and introducing role models through an intranet, supporting for working includes holding seminars for woman who are pregnant or on maternity leave and introducing a system or part employment. As a result, the number of employee and nearly all of tem return to the workforce. Because airport service industry needs have a large female workforce, including cabin attendants and airport passenger service staff. Besides, airport service industry also needs to hire women for career track administrative and maintenance positions and flight crews and working to increase the percentage of women in management positions.

Better work life balance is also needed to satisfy airport service industry staff. Besides, airport service industry also needs to hire women for career track administrative and maintenance positions and flight crews and working to increase the percentage of women in management positions. Because airport job duty is common needed to be shift duty. Hence, the working time is flexible time to work when new employees decide to attribute to airport service career. However, due to many passengers need, so airport service workers need to work overtime hours. But, commonly, who do not hope to work overtime often. So, airport management needs to create an comfortable and enjoyable working environment in which each new or old employee can rethink whose own working style to contribute will help vitalize society, companies and individuals.

How to leverage technology to improve employee engagement? Nowadays, employee engagement has evolved from a relatively unknown trend to a term in common usage, which leads itself to a variety of forms and levels of understanding. Employee engagement is about the ability of leaders to inspire their people around the way forward at the desired pace, involving a planned communication effort that is integrated with all the other leadership and change activities. Employee engagement is the emotional commitment the employee has to the organization and its goals. However, technology can play an important role in making engagement a practical part of everyday work. As companies move towards a digital workplace, understanding the impact of technology on employee engagement is critical.

What is the digital workplace? The digital workplace is the digital environment in which staff work, and a place to find corporate knowledge. It includes a collection of election tools that enable productive, effective, work from anywhere. In the future, according to the workplace of the future survey by Teknion corporation predicted 88% of companies offer their workforce personal devices, such as smartphones and tablets. Nearly 90% of companies plan to increase their investment in productivity enabling technologies, such as voice activation and video conferencing by 20 15 year. Organizations are seeking the workplace as which search for ways to be more efficient, more collaborative and reduce their physical workplace to realizing higher levels of productivity with their workforce. So, it seems digital workplace can assist to raise performance. Two important reasons why new technology tools will be represent great return on investment for internal use with employees.

The first reason is technology helps us comment with and engage remote or disconnected employees, those with little or no computer or internet access during their work time . The second reason is peer-to-peer engagement and using technology can drive the generation of more ideas, which drives innovation and improvement to produce in any workplace. So, creating an actionable roadmap that fully technology in any organization's staff engagement initiatives can improve bottom line performance. So, technology can assist organization to measure employee engagement, connect disconnected workers, encourage collaboration and social interaction.

I assure engagement lies in sound decision making and action, then driving good decision making and action should be a communicator's core strategy. Many communicators are already doing good work to drive action. Then, good decision making is driven, in part, by the availability f good information. Even employees who are less digital connected at work can contribute great ideas that improve that work situation and organizational productivity. Examples, of ways technology helps to that such as: one employee posts about a project who is working on, another employee in an office on the other side ot the world sees the post and realizes who is working on a similar project. If the two teams combine their effort, who can solve the problem and the company gets a global solution. So, corporate internet is a new digital workplace tools. To effectively solve challenge as making the right information available to the right people at the right time. Organizations must begin by clearly identifying the core types of information that must be shared to engage employee and bring about maximum organizational benefit.

What critical organizational information should all employees access? What types of knowledge are suitable for collaboration? What informational exist today and how are these pockets of information affecting business performance? When analyzing your environment for knowledge sharing, take the time to understand knowledge sharing objectives and how to get employees on information that empowers them to be more successful and therefore more engaged. Remember, anyone can serve in this knowledge management role as long as who are contributing relevant and engaging information.

When looking at any new technology to improve organization knowledge transfer and employee engagement for your employees you should consider the following questions: How does the proposed technology create for information sharing? Are they create for information sharing? Are they easy to use for people of all levels of the organization? How does the technology solution you are examine help employees get work accomplished? This is especially important when examining enterprise social technologies. How can the technology provide more information about company vision, people, business processes. How effectively does the technology support key organizational scenarios, such as identifying the best talent for a particular department or initiative? For example, hospital environment can give conversation about the patient benefits of a new in-room online information display at a hospital.

● How can influence organizational positive behaviors ?
Nowadays, there are key forces are affecting daily organizational behaviors and continuing challenges, such as staff structure (work relationship), technology (resources inputs)are needs to transform to with people work and affects the tasks that who perform, environment (internal and external) factors influence the attitudes of staff, affect working conditions and

provide competition for resources and power. So, based on these four forces, managers need to face the different challenges, such as managing chances in a global environment, managing ethical issues at work.

How to raise staff performance to satisfy clients' needs? Customer service and satisfaction is not limited to the private sector, public sector also needs , e.g. education reform, private, managed case. So, staff need have excellent performance to raise quality of service to satisfy students, patients etc. needs. Why organizations focus on customer satisfaction. Business monitor customer satisfaction in order to determine how to increase customer base, customer loyalty, revenue, profit, market share and survival. Besides, government needs to monitor customer satisfaction to achieve citizen needs. What is customer satisfaction? Customer satisfaction can be experienced in a variety of situations and connected to both products and services. It is a highly personal assessment that is greatly affected by customer expectations, satisfaction also is based on the customer's experience of both contact with the organization , the moment of truth and personal outcomes. Private sector means it is as one who receives significant added value as well as public sector means it is to whose bottom line. However, customer satisfaction differs depending on the situation and the product or service. A client may be satisfied with a product or service on experience, a purchase decision, a salesperson, store, service provider or an attitude. So, staff performance can influence or client's decision to choose to buy the product or consume the service indirectly. For example, in hospital organization , patient surveys often ask customers to rate their providers and experiences in response to detailed questions, such as " How well did your physicians keep you informed?" These surveys provide "actions" data that reveal obvious steps for improvement.

Client satisfaction is highly personal assessment that is greatly influenced by individual expectation. In the public sector, the definition of client satisfaction is often linked to both the personal interaction with the service provider and the outcomes experiences by service users. For example, satisfaction with client worker interaction whether in person, by phone, or by mail or by email communication, satisfaction with the support payment , e.g. its accuracy and timeliness and satisfaction with the effect of child support enforcement on the child. For hospital organization, staff performance need have these service quality factors to raise or improve whose service satisfaction experience to whose patients (clients), e.g. timeliness and convenience, personal attention, reliability and dependability, employee competence and professionalism, empathy, responsiveness, assurance, availability and tangible, such as physical facilities and equipment and the appearance of the personnel.

Satisfaction and engagement are two important distinct measurements that provide valuable and actionable insights into the workforce. The problem is that how many organizations still view them as one and the same thing. As a result, they may be missing critical opportunities to foster the kind of workforce engagement that drives innovation, boosts performance and increases competitive success. However, some organizations think which don't have to worry about engagement because turnover is how and employees seem satisfied when employee satisfaction is important to maintaining a positive work environment. Is it enough to help you retain top performers and drive bottom line impact? Probably not, by focusing more employee engagement, organizations are more likely to maintain a strong, motivated workforce that is willing to expand extra effort, drive business goals and deliver a return on HR's talent management investment. How to achieve actionable strategies for maximizing workforce engagement and subsequently, driving higher performance across the organization. It addresses critical questions, such as: Do you want satisfied employees or engaged employees? Which has a greater impact on the organization's bottom line? What are some proven techniques for addressing both satisfaction and engagement? Employee satisfaction can typically measured through surveys to gather opinions about HR related issues like bonus programs, benefits and work/life balance. Some employee satisfaction can refer to how employees feel, that happiness about their job and conditions, such as compensation, benefits, work environment, career development opportunities. On the other hand, engagement refers to employees commitment and connection to work as measured by the amount of discretinary effort, who are willing to expand discretionary effort, who are willing to expand on behalf of their employer. High engaged employees go above and beyond the core responsibilities outlines in their job descriptions, innovating and thinking outside the box to move their organizations forward, much like volunteers are willing to give their fine and energy to support a cause about which they are truly passionate.

Can an organization have a satisfied employee who isn't engaged? Chances is an engaged employee is also a satisfied employee. However, it is certainly possible to have a satisfied employee a with a low engagement level. That's why focusing on satisfaction without addressing engagement is unlikely to foster the kind of expect workforce performance that drives business results. Why do organizations need to care about their workforce engagement level? The primary goal of a business is to make money, even non profit organizations exist to fund their specific causes. Many studies have linked organizations need to get employees at all levels focused on driving revenue. Also which indicates to link employee engagement to workforce preference, customer satisfaction, productivity absenteeism, turnover. Employee engagement is a concept that is rooted in science and at the most fundamental level reflects the human condition itself.

It makes sense that this human motivation process would apply in the workplace just as in other areas of life. By motivating employees beyond basic satisfaction to achieve higher levels of engagement. HR professionals have more significantly impact business outcomes and drive bottom line results. Top-performing organizations understand that measuring employees' contentment levels and emotional commitment to the organization on a regular basis can put them at a competitive advantage. Since satisfaction measures on employee happiness with current job and security opportunities to use skills and abilities, the organization's financial stability, relationship with immediate supervisor, compensation and benefits. In general, these factors can contribute to job satisfaction, such as job security, opportunities to use skills and abilities, organization's financial stability, relationship with immediate supervisor compensation and benefit, communication between employees and senior management, the work itself, autonomy and independence, management's recognition of employee performance. However, fact engagement condition can have these difference with job satisfaction, such as relationship with co-workers, opportunities to use skills and abilities relationship with immediate supervisor, contribution of work to organization's business goal, meaningfulness of job, variety of work, overall corporate cultures. In general, staff tend to receive more pleasure and satisfaction from what who do if who are in jobs or roles that match both their interests and skills if staff feel who are making meaningful contributions to whose jobs, their organizations do society as a whole, they tend to be more engages. Staff want to be recognized and rewarded for their contributions. Rewards and recognition come in many forms, including competitive compensation packages, a healthy work/life balance, or sales trips etc. benefits. So, lack of motivation will affect productivity. In addition, a number of point to low morale: declining productivity, higher incidence of absenteeism and friend, increasing defective products higher number of accidents or a higher level of waste materials and scrapes. How much money (salary) will you give to your employee to satisfy whose needs? However, staff's needs differ some can be motivated by opportunity for growth and development, job security, good working condition more than high salary.

In conclusion, as a manager, if you want to develop and encourage good employee performance, and good performance comes from strong employee motivation. But managers can't motivate employee. Motivation is an internal state, like emotions and attitudes, that only the individual can control. Managers can however, create a workplace environment to attempt to motivate staff. Nowadays, workplace is affected by a number of factors, including a decreasing emphasis on money, an increasing amount of work, an increasing need to work together in teams. Hence, employers concern to consider these above different psychological factors which can influence employee's individual behavior to perform efficiently in any organization.

Reference

Branham, L. (2005). The 7 Hidden Reasons Employees Leave: How To Recognize The Subtle Signs And Act Before Its Too Late. New York, NY: Amacom.

Clark, R.E. (1998). Motivating Performance, Performance Improvement, 37 (8), 39-47.

Clark, R.E. & Estes, F. (2002). Turning Research Into

Results: A Guide To Selecting The Right Performance Solutions. Atlanta, G.A: CEP Press.

Johnsrud, L.K. and Rosser, V.J., 1999. College and

University Midlevel Administrators:

Explaining and improving their morale. The

review of higher education, 22(2), pp. 121-141.

Kristof, A.C. 1996. Person-organization fit: An

Integrative Review of its conceptualizations, measurement and implications. Personnel psychology, 49(1), pp.1-49.

Larrabee J.H. Janney M.A., Ostrow C.L., Withrow M.L.,

Hobbs G.R. And Burant C. (2003) Predicting

registered nurse job satisfaction and intent

to leave., Journal of nursing administration,

33 (5), 271-283.

Shenkel, R. & Gardner, C. (2004), " Five ways to retain good staff", Family Management, Now-Dec. , pp.57-59.

World at work (2009). Telework trend lines. Retrieved from http://www.workingfromanywhere.org/ News/Trend lines_2009.pdf

VI

How to learn qualificative research interviewing in order to raise efficiency and effectiveness

I assume that if the interviewer can learn whose what errors are in order to let him/her to review from past every time interview experience, then he/she can know how to improve future every time interview, e.g. controlling or managing time arrangment to every new interview process, asking what knids of questions to let the interviewer to attempt to answer for any kinds of position applocation suitation, how to make judge whose feedbacks or answers to any kinds of interviewing questions to be more reasonable in order to select the most right applicants to improve the interviewer's interviewing efficiency and make the more effective interviewing consequences, e.g. when the interview has 100 applicants or more on that day , and it has only one to three interviewer(s) number. Hence, time controlling and managing and how to ask interview quetions will be one value considerable questions to the interviewer(s), if the interviewer does not want to waste time to make wrong judgement to select the applicant(s)

who is(are) not the most right applicant(s) to do the position(s). Hence, how to learn the qualitative research interviewing, it will be one value question to any interviews for whose organizational economic benefits, because their interviewing behavior will influence their organizations time and resource and human resource lose or waste to do other important or urgent tasks every day, when they use the limited working time to concentrate on the interviewing and selection task only , but on more time to do other efficient and effective interviewing tasks. So, it brings this question: How can the interviewer learn past interviewing experience in order to improve next every time qualitative research interviewing consequence?

Steinar, K & Svend, B. (2009, p.2) explains thatdifferent forms of interviews serve different purposes: Journalistic position application interviews are means of recording and reporting important events in society, theapeutic position application. Interviews seek to improve debilitating suitations in people's times, and research interviews have the purpose of producing knowledge. Hence, the interviewer needs know whether what kinds of position, the applicant is applying, e.g. above different kinds of professional jobs. They need the applicant owns the kind of professional knowledge and technique and educational level to do the kind of professional job, in order to do the kind of position more proficient. So, above of all these kinds of professional job interviews, they have need have these basic application requirement to let the interviewer to select, but how to ask different kinds of interviewing questions to every applicant, he/ she can follow whom educational background and owning related working related experience to choose the interviewer ought ask him/her, the application what kinds of interviewing questions in order to let him/her to answer or give feedbacks in order to make more accurate selective decision to every applicant in fact.

The research interview is based on the conversations of daily life and is a professional conversation to any interviewer's daily interviewing task. It is an interview, where knowledge is constructed in the inter action between the interviewer and the interviewee. Any one interviewer needs to know an interview is a conservation that has a structure and a purpose and it becomes a careful questioning and listening approach with the purpose of training thoroughly tested knowledge.

The research interview is not a conversation between equal partners because the inteviewing researcher needs to define and control the situation for interview. The positive application interview researcher needs to introduce the topic of the job interview and also critically , follows up on the subject's answer to hir /her interviewing questions. So, it is one time spending tasks to any interviewers, when any interview needs to be carried on. I shall indicate the main interview learning points as below:

The first interview learning point is any job interviewing is an active process where interviewer and interviewee through their relationship produce social knowledge. Interview knowledge is product in a conservational relation. The conception interview knowledge presented to contrast with a methodogical positivison conception of knowledge as given facts to be quantified, e.g. in one journalist position application interview, the interviewer asks the same question to ten applicants. The question: How do you have more confidence to apply your past journal writing working experience and knowledge to do this journalist job? When these ten applicants listened this question. They will have different feeling to answer this question. Hence, the interviewer can follow their different answers or feedbacks to compare these 10 applicants' consumers to judge whether whose answers can have more reasonable to be accepted as well as the interviewer also needs to record how much time , that they need to answer this question. Hence, a conception of conception of research interviewing is as a rule governed method, it will lead to different job application interview practices than an inderstanding of research interviewing as a tool, where the quality of the kind of job interview knowledge is more important to comapre the skills and the personal judgement of the interviewer.

The another interview learning point is the interviewer needs to understand whose interview tasks is a semi-structured life and he/she needs to attempt to understand the applicant's lived eveyday world from his/her subjects' own perspectives, when the interviewee attempts to answer the interviewer's any interviewing questions by whose owning methods. This kind of interview seeks to obtain descriptions of the interviewees' lived world wit respect to interpretation of the meaning of the described phenomena. It comes close to an everyday conservation, such as the interiewer's everyday asking interviewing questions and listening the interviewer's every job applicant's answers or feedbacks, but when the interviewer assumes whose interview tasks, it needs to involve a specific approach and technique, it is semi-structured and it is neither an open everyday conservation nor a closed questionnaire between the job interviewer himself/herself and whose any job applicants. It is conducted according to an intervew guide that focuses on certain themes and that may include suggested questions. The job application interview is usually transcribed, and the written text and sound recording together constitute the materials for the subsequence analysis of meaning after every time interview. It aims to let the interviewer himself/herself can make more accurate judgement to select whom is the most right applicant to the job.

Steinar, K. & Svend, B. (2009, p.28) indicates one qualitative research interview has any one of these twelve aspects characteristics. They incude as below :

The topic of qualitative interview is the every day lived world of the interviewee and the interviewer his/her relation to it; the interview seeks to interpret the meaning of central themes in the life world of the subject; the interviewer needs to register and interpret the meaning of what is said as well as how it is said between the interviewer himself/herself and the interviewee(s) in every time interview; the interview seeks qualitative knowledge expressed in normal language, it does not aim at quantification, the interview attempts to obtain open descriptions of different aspects of the subjects life worlds, descriptions of specific situations and general opinions , the interviewer needs to exhibit openness to new and unexpected phenomena, the interview is focused on particular themes, it is neither strictly stim-structured with standardized questions, interviewee statements can sometimes be reflected, contradictions is the world the subject live in, the process of being interviewed may produce new insights and awareness, and the subject may in the course of the interview, come to change the interviewer's descriptions and meanings about a theme, different interviewers can produce different statements can produce different statements on the same themes , depending on their sensitivity to and knowledge of the interview topic, the knowledge obtained is produced through the interpersonal interaction in the interview, a well carried out research interview can be a rare and enriching experience for the interviewee, who may obtain new insights into his/her life situation.

The final interview learning point is that the interviewer also needs to have ethical issues in research interviewing, to control or manage himself/herself interview behavior. Ethics is basic to an interview inquiry. It situations of conflict, the applicant's selective decision about which rules to follow with to a large extent depend upon the interview researcher's experience and personal judgement experienced interviewers. The interviewing skills, the knowledge, and the interviewer personal judgements necessary for conducting a qualitative interview of a high quality require extensive job interview training. The flexible , content and content-related skills of interviewing are acquired by doing interviews. Whereas, the interview of questiond can be communicated verbally, other aspects of interview skills, such as the kinds of interview questions, sensitive listening and the establishing of good environment in the interview situation all these ethic factors are very important to influence one efficient and effective interview achievement.

In conclusion, to achieve one qualitative interview learning method in success. The interviewer needs to learn, such as one good interview practice consists of more than carrying out practical act , it also involves a situated judgement of what knowledge and techniques to apply when acting in a given interview situation, and when every interview is needed to carry on with different goals and values that interview demand careful choice. Hence, a research interviewing is learned by practicing interviewing, preferably within a personal interview experiene of whether the interviewee needed to use how much time to answer this interview question(s) in order to make more effective and qualitative accurate and fair researching selective decision to employ whom is the most right applicant to do as above this journalist position example among these journlist applicants.

Reference

Steinar, K & Svend, B. (2009) interviews learning the craft of qualitative research interviewing, US: SAGE publications, Inc. pp. 2, pp.28.

VII

How to apply psychological methods to predict employee individual productive efficiency and service performance

It has one interesting question concerns whether organization's in-house training management and/or human resource training course program has close relationship to influence the reducing or raising employee individual productive efficiency and better or worse service performance consequence. I shall recommend that any organizations can apply psychological methods to judge whether they need to implement their facility management department to change their working environment to be better in order to let their employees feel comfortable to work to raise productive efficiency or implement training course program to let employees to learn in order to raise productive efficiency.

How to apply psychological methods to evaluate whether the organization has need to implement in-house facility management service and/or any employee train courses program? I shall explain as below:

Some essential concepts in psychological research concerns employees' raising productive efficiency and improving service performance may include as below:

● Cause means something which results in an effect, e.g. The organization's employees overall service performance is worse (effect) and/or overall productive efficiencies are worse (effect), it is due to the poor working environment factor and/or lacking effective training courses program provision (cause).

● Action or condition means that the organization's employees often perform worse (action), it is due to they feel worse working environment (condition) to influence their emotions are negative.

● Data means that the information from which are drawn and conclusions reached. For example, the organization gather much data concerns workplace environment variable facilities factors, e.g. enough air conditioners, clean canteen facilities, large warehouse space allocation available etc. variable data as well as training course contents data. Then it will analyze all these both kinds of data to make the accurate conclusion reached to make the more accurate conclusion reached to judge whether its employees overall worse productive efficiencies and/or worse service performance effect is due to either worse workplace working environment and/or lacking enough training work-related course programs provision to let them to learn.

In any large organization's improving employee performance and/or raising productive efficient research. A lot of data are collected in numerical form , e.g. how many employees feel their workplace environment is satisfactory or comfortable? The workplace environment comfortable and satisfactory feeling rank:

1 means the most comfortable,

2 means more comfortable,

3 means worse comfortable,

4 means the worst comfortable,

But it is equally viable to use data in the form of text for an analysis and randomized experiment means a type of research in which participants in research are allocated at random by chance to an experimental or control condition. For example, when one organization needs 20 employees to do one performance improving experiment in one day 9 working hours. The 10 employees are arranged to manufacture watch product in one large warehouse space available and more cool temperature feeling working environment factory. The other 10 employees are arranged to manufacture the same kind of watch product in one small warehouse space available and less cool temperature feeling working environment factory. Hence, their watch manufacturing skills must be same proficient level, due to they manufacture the same kind of watch and the two factories' equipment supplies are same number and their qualities are the new purchase, and these two factories' worker number is same , the two variable factors are different , it is only that one factory's space is large size and the another factory's space is small size as well as one factory's temperature is much cooler, but the another factory's temperature is less cooler. This organization's one day working hours experiment aims to research whether these two factories' warehouses' space size variable factor and temperature variable factor whether they can influence these two groups of 20 workers overall productive efficiencies to bring the much difference of watch manufacturing number of the day. For example, if the large space available and much cooler warehouse's 10 employees can manufacture more than 500 watch number in the day. Otherwise, the small space available and less cooler warehouse's 10 employees can only manufacture less than 300 watch number in the day. Then, the organization can judge the conclusion concerns whether the better or worse workplace environment will influence its employee individual emotion to manufacture its watch number.

All above these elements are each employee performance psychological research needs. Any employee psychological researches are needed to evaluate the evidence. Employee individual performance psychology is not simply about learning what conclusions have been reached on a particular topic. It is perhaps more important to find out and carefully evaluate the evidence which has led to these conclusion. For example, in the newspapers and on television, one comes findings from advertising influence consumers (audiences) media research. IS it simply to accept what the newspaper or television report claims or world it be better media choice to be advertised to check the original research in order to evaluate what the best advertisement media choice to attract customers (audiences') attention actually meant?

The evaluation of employee performance improving evidence involves examining the general findings that the employee psychological research is making about an issue and the information or data that are relevant to this finding, e.g. The organization has not implement any training courses to let employee to learn, (it is the issue), the organization discovers many employee individual productive efficiency is worse, it is the information, this organization will gather different variable data, e.g. the equipment number whether is enough to supply to them to apply to work, the equipment quality whether is good or bad, new or old, the worker individual proficient skill level is high or low or their working related skillful experience is long or short years. Then, it can make more accurate analysis to find whether the lacking enough training courses program to be supplied to let them to learn any work-related skills, whether this variable factor is the major variable factor to influence their performance to be worse. For example, if this organization had enough equipment number supply and all are new and these workers' overall proficient skillful level is high and they own many years working experience about this kind of tasks. Then, it can judge the lacking training course program implementation is not the major factor to influence their performance to be worse, due to their performance ought not need to be improved. SO, it ought have other variable factors to influence their performance to be worse suddenly.

Then, the organization needs to check whether the evidence or data support the finding or whether the finding goes beyond what could be confidently concluded. However, in any employee performance psychological research, there is nothing wrong with speculation as such since hypotheses.

What is causal explanation in employee performance psychological research view point? Dennis , H & Duncan, C. (2005, pp.9-10), they stated one prisoner suicide risk case example of causal explanation, a psychologist who wishes to predict suicide risk in prisoners does not have to know why the causes of suicide among prisoners. So, if research shows that being in prison for the first time is the strongest predictor of suicide, then this is a possible predictor. It is irrelevant whether the predictor is in itself the direct cause of suicide. Hence, the two authors assume that in general, the prisoners choose to suicide in prisons. Usually, they are the first time to enter the prison. Because the two authors assume the psychologist does not know what the reasons cause prisoners choose to do suicide behavior in prison, because it is possible that these first time prisoners who feel difficult to adapt to live in prisons' strange environment, they afraid to be fright or hurt by another/other prisoners' hurt in prison, they also feel alone , when they can not live with their families together forever. SO, the reasons of not adaptable living in prison, which is possible to cause the first time prisoners to choose to suicide in prisons. Hence, the first time prisoners suicide in prisons, it is one assumption , when the psychologist does not know what reasons cause prisoners suicide in prisons in general. Such as employee performance research, organizations usually do not know what reasons cause their employees' overall performance to be worse suddenly, it is possible that their families relationship is worse, or they feel wage/salary level is too low to compare the industry's average salary/wage level, or they feel their company's promotion chance is less, or they hope to change another new job. However, the organization needs to assume that poor workplace environment and/or lacking effective training course program , these both factors will cause its employees' performance to be worse suddenly. Thus, causal explanation view point, it will need to be considered to any organizations when they need to do any employee performance psychological research.

● Aims and hypotheses in employee performance psychological research

The possible aims of employee psychological research is to examine research objectives as three research aspects, such as below:

1. Descriptive or exploratory studies, it concerns case studies are reports that describe a particular case in detail, for example, the case study research aim can be conceived as investigating the factors that how they can be created, to find what factors cause the consequences which can be the psychological research aim. Such as employee performance psychological research case, when the organization needs to investigate whether in general, some employee individual productive efficiency is worse, the causes are due to themselves family relationship or lacking money spending or changing new job desire etc. non –related its organizational weaknesses factors or it's organizational weaknesses factors, such as poor working environment , lacking enough facilities supply, or poor manger individual attitude, or lacking enough training to improve their efficiency. So, when the organization discover its employees perform worse suddenly. It needs to gather data to investigate whether what are the major factors to cause its employees perform worse suddenly.

2. Evaluation or outcome studies, it aims to test the effectiveness of a particular feature. This kind of research often seeks to develop theory to explain why the outcome occurrence. It simply concentrates on the consequences of certain activities without attempting to test theoretical or ideas to explain how any why the consequences are caused. For employee performance research case example, when the organization knows its

employees' overall performance is worse, e.g. this month car manufacturing number is less than 50 % to compare last month . The less than 50% car manufacturing number to this month, it is the effectiveness feature. The organization expects to find the reasons why this month's car manufacturing number reduces less than 50% to compare last month suddenly. It is possible due to the machines qualities are worse and old obsolete when they are used to manufacture cars long term, needed new technologies , e.g. artificial intelligent manufacturing robots, employees feel tried to work, when they often need to overtime to work or the employees number is not enough. SO, its poor productive efficient consequence must not be caused by poor manufacturing workplace environment or lacking enough training to workers both factors. It is due to the organization itself resource shortage problem. Then, the organization needs to gather different category of data to evaluate whether why its overall employee's performance is worse to compare last month suddenly.

3. This kind of research is meta-analysis studies. It aims to summarize and analyze the results of the range of studies which have investigated a particular topic . It is in a systematic and structured way using statistical techniques. These trends may be used to calculate what is known as an effect size. This is the size of the trend in the data adjusted for the variability in the data. For employee performance psychological research example, when the organization expects to find whether the other similar competitors between owning training department and lacking training department , what are the advantages will be possible to bring or/and what are the disadvantages will be possible to bring as well as whether it has need to implement one training department to bring the possible advantages to itself. Then , it needs a systematic and structured way using statistical techniques. These trends may be used to calculate what is known as an effect size. This is the size of the trend in the data adjusted for the variability in the data for its reference sources. It aims to analyze whether the training department is needed to bring what the good or bad influences to its similar competitors in order to help itself to make the judgement whether it ought need to set up one training department or not.

● What the employee performance research aim?

The employee performance researcher needs to have an understanding of what purposes the research will serve and how likely it is to serve these purposes. The employee performance researcher needs to be able to present the aims of their studies with enough clarity to justify just why the research was done in the way in which it was done. More importantly, the aims of the research need to be clearly justified by providing their rational.

In conclusion, justifying the aims research can involve: Explaining the relevance of the research to what is already known about the topic as well as reference to the wider social situation, e.g. competitors' productive efficiency and organizational development growth situation for research, employee performance psychology research is often a response to the concerns of whole society by government, social institutions, such as the legal and educational system, business organization.

● What are employee psychological research hypotheses?

The use of hypotheses is more common in employee psychological performance research than in concerning , such as sociology, economics and other related subjects. A hypothesis does not have to be true since the point of research is to examine the support or its aim is for the hypothesis, e.g. One car manufacturing organization assumes that all first time new car manufacturing employees , they lack enough skills to manufacture its different kinds of cars , so it assumes that they all need to be trained to raise their car manufacturing skills to be proficient, if it expects that they can raise productive efficiency in short time, e.g. one month. It implies that it needs have one training department to provide effective car manufacturing training courses to let them to learn satisfactorily if their car manufacturing technique can be improved in short time. SO, it has both assumptions, the first is all car manufacturing workers' skills are not enough as well as the second is that an effective training courses program can improve their car manufacturing skills in short time in order to raise productive efficiency after one month.

A hypothesis does not have to be true, such as car manufacturing firm case, since the point of research is to examine the support of it's aim is for the hypothesis. So, hypotheses are assumptions to link to the aims of the study. Such as the car manufacturing firm aims to raise its car manufacturing worker's skills to be proficient after one month, so it assumes that its all new workers' skills are not proficient and it is one an effective training courses program can improve their skills to manufacture the increasing car number after one month in possible. So, it does not concern other variable factors will influence their car manufacturing performance.

However, hypotheses can contain three variables: Attitude importance, attitude similarity, interpersonal attraction variables. These assumptions concern to research the firm's employee personal individual working attitude can be either similar, e.g. many employees' working attitude is positive or liking to work or many employees' working attitude is negative or disliking to work, or interpersonal attraction , e.g. many employees can be influenced to reduce productive efficiencies , due to the poor performance of employees' personal influence, or attitude importance in a group of student's learning behavior, such as business organization case, the team employees' overall working performance behavior can influence the other team members' working behavior obviously.

So, this psychological research can assume the Classroom students' learning attitude can be either similar to hard to learn, or these students can influence interpersonal attraction to influence themselves learning attitude together in classroom or all these students' feeling which is their whole classroom's all student their learning attitudes are very important factor to influence themselves whole learning behaviors in classroom. So, such as any organizations' employees , organizations can also assume that many employee individual performance can be influenced to perform better or worse when they need to cooperate to work in different teams working environment together.

● What are variables, concepts and measures meaning to any employee performance psychological research

The variable means a key concept in psychological research. A variable is anything which varies and can be measured , e.g. the organization's overall employees performance or productive efficiencies can be raised or decreased the product number in any time, it is tangible, such as manufacturing number's increasing or decreasing number. These is a distinction between a concept and how it is measured. Otherwise, hypothetical is not variable, but theoretical or conceptual inventions, which explains what we can observe in our psychological research. It is feeling and intangible.

Variables are what we create when we try to measure concepts. So, we will use the term variable without discussing the idea in any great details. Variables are the things what we measure. They are not exactly the same thing as the concepts that we use when trying to develop theories about something. For example, if one social psychological student wished to measure social influence how to influence people's behaviors in the country, the social psychological student might so, so in a number of different ways, such as number of people who disagree with a participant in s study.

The use of concepts of independent variable and dependent variables was being encouraged by experimental psychologists to replace the response. The term variable tool prominence between psychologists concludes psychological phenomena in terms of the variables familiar from statistics. In this way, psychological phenomena in terms of the variables familiar from statistics.

Dennis, H & Duncan, C. (2005, pp.39-40) indicated variables in psychology can include these sample different types: causal variable, it is only psychological domain. It is not possible to establish cause and effect sequences , simply on the basic of statistics, e.g. the organization can not find what factors cause its employees overall performance to be worse. It can only find data gathering of all similar competitors' overall worse performance analysis; hypothetical construct , it is only psychological domain, it is not really a form of variable , but an unobservable psychological structure or process , which explains observable findings, e.g. the organization assumes all new employees' overall productive efficiencies will be worse to compare the old employees and it assumes that an effective training program can improve the new employees' performance in short time; independent variable includes psychological or statistical variable in the dependent variables. As a psychological independent variable has a causal effect on the dependent variable. This is not the case when considered as a statistical concept. Ratio variable is only statistical domain, it measured on an numerical scale which has a proper new point. This allows the researcher to make ratio statements, such as person it is twice as tall as person is, such as organization's performance research, e.g. this month, this organization's manufacturing number can raise to manufacture more than three times to compare last month.

However, it is given close relationships between psychology and statistics, many variables do not readily talk into just one
of these categories. This is sometimes because psychologists have taken statistical terminology and observed it into their professional vocabulary to refer to slightly different things.
It brings one interesting question concerns variable: How
can a variable be the independent variable of the causal direction of the relationship between two variables is not know? E.g. When one organization believes that there is possible to cause worse performance, due to either lacking effective training or worse workplace environment, how

it can prove that these two variables both can influence
their employees' worse performance in the same time.

For example, variables which can be calculated number
and which are characteristic of the participant , subject variables , variables can be example: How old the person is, how intelligent, they are, how anxious , they are etc. when
the organization employ any one of its employees. All these variables may be described aas the independent variable by some researchers. Such as this psychological research what characteristics the participant, it can not be explained how the causal direction of the relationship between the participant's age and whether his age has relationship to cause his intelligent level, e.g. when he is younger, then he is more intelligent, so when he is older, he will be less intelligent, however, these two variables are not known by the psychological researcher. Such as the organization's employee individual age variable, which will influence their intelligent level in order to learn training courses more easily to bring effect of the raising productive efficiency in short time or the employee is younger and he is health, so the worse workplace can not influence his productive efficiency to be worse. Hence, in the organization case, it will need to try to predict what the value is of the criterion variable to the participant's psychological research from the values of the predictor variable or variables in order to decide whether what are /is the main factor(s) to influence its organizational performance.

● What is quantitative variables mean?

When we measure a quantitative variable, the numbers or values we assign to each person or case represent increasing levels of the variable. These numbers are known as scores since they represent amounts of something. For example, in one quiz game to research whether whom game player is
more clever, the independent variable might be age and the dependent variable may be scores on a quiz game or some other measure of general knowledge, older people do better
on the general knowledge quiz game. So, age itself, is not responsible for higher scores on the quit game. Otherwise, these may be more than one variable, e.g. educational experiences to raise the quit game player's skill to earn higher scores to win any quiz game competition. So, it seems that younger age quit game player must not earn higher scores to compare the older age quiz game player.

Age factor is not the main factor . Otherwise, education all experience will prove any quiz game players' skill to raise quiz playing skill to learn how to win the quiz competition more easily. So, age and clever is not the main factor to assist quiz game player to win easily. Learning experience will be one main psychological factor to assist the quiz game player to win any quiz competition.

It concludes there is an individual effect of age to influence the quiz game players' on the scores on the quiz. Otherwise, these may be more than mediator variable , e.g. educational experiences to raise the game competition. So, it seems that younger age quiz game player must not earn higher scores to compare the older age quiz game player. Age factor is not the main factor. Such as employee psychological performance research, organizations ought assume many different factors, include the non-related organizational as well as related organizational factors in order to find whether its organization ought need to implement effective training or/ and implement facility management strategy to improve workplace environment to achieve the raising productive efficiency or improving performance aim. Because each factors will be possible dependent or independent.

Reference

Dennis, H & Duncan, C. (2005), Introduction to research methods in psychology , 2 edition: New York, US Person Prentice Hall, pp. 9-10., pp. 39-40.

Human resource department and
organizational performance
relationship

In any large organizations, whether human resource department can assist organizations to raise employees' effective and productive performance, instead of its basic main functions, such as selection, interviewing , performance management, reward management, training functions. I shall follow these several aspects to analysize whether human resource can assist to any organizations to raise efficiency and productive performance in possible. They may include these several aspects to analyze: The impact of training factor influences performance, the impact of recruitment and selection factor influences performance, the impact of facility management environment factor influences performance , the impact of reward and performance management factor influences performance.

Firstly, I shall explain how and why training provision factor may influence performance. In organization, training is one kind of method to assist employees to learn. The organization's technique and culture. Any organizations expect to survival, they will need employees to work or grow in one organizational learning and creation of learning environment in order to raise their skills, techniques and knowledge of level to work efficiently.

Hence , one learning organization needs employees to change mindset knowledge and values as well as improved organizational performance. Organizational learning may be any one of these processes occurring and organizational levels. Individual learning means to change in individual's knowledge, beliefs and ideas. Learning means to share understanding and interaction among employees.

Hence, in any organizations, they belong to this kind of learning team , employees need learn together in their deparments as well as organizational learning , it requires something more than shared understanding among employees, different departments' employees need to share understanding with other departments' employees. At this level of learning organizational factors need to be linked together and to individual and group learning to facilities organizational learning.

It brings this question: Can organizational learning bring the organizational overall performance improvement consequence? In fact, in any training, when employees attempt to apply the different training methods to solve their tasks difficulties. They will be possible to encounter fundamental barriers should be identified and removed. It seems that in their process of encountering barriers and finding solving methods to remove. This is one learning process to let them to attempt to accept problems and threats, and train them to learn to analyze which is the best method to solve the problem from training learning knowledge.

It is possible to raise employee individual efficiency from the training and learning error review process. The reason is that performance is the process of determining the efficiency of past activities. Organizational performance is in general concept means to how organizational operations are performed. Organizational performance measurement determines whether the organization has been successful as well as it is much discussed , but little understood.

However, there are other factors that influence organizational performance either directly or indirectly. For example, learning culture is one the important internal factors affecting organizatonal performance. A creative company needs to employ high levels of organizational learning and could use the information more efficient employees to work more than one non-creative company. So, it seems that effective training may create high creative learning culture to increase the high creative level of employees number to attribute a positive high levels of learning and financial and knowledge performance to the organization.

Hence, management tends to follow approaches that may guarantee organizational success. Since, any one organizational learning training chance provision is considered as an important factor in the efficiency of dynamic organizations. Learning and training is a process that brings about changes in performace through acqusition of knowledge and experience as well as training. Learning at the individual level includes changing in skills, attitudes , knowledge and values of individual employees. For example, a sport professional needs to be trained to learn the kind of sport knowledge from his/her sport trainer every day. So, sport practice and sport learning techniqie will assist the sport professional to raise whose individual sport skill in order to win the award achievement. For another example, one teacher can be trained and practice his/her teaching skill from his/her university's education course. So, university organization can provide skill to raise teacher teaching effort in order to improve whose teaching performance and adapt whose teaching career more easily. Hence, some occupations , such as teacher, sport professional etc. they ought need to be trained by teachers in order to help their organizations to improve overall performance more easily than without training provision.

Why can training learning provision internal variable factor impact organization's overall performance? Human resource is the main capital in any organizations. Efficiency and productivity of any organization is depended on the behavior and performance of its staffs and employees. Any training learning provision can being innovation benefit to the organization. The concept of innovation means a important enabling tool to create value and competitive advantage within organizations in a changing environment with increasing complexities. In fact, the starting point for innovation strongly relies on knowledge, expertise and commitment of human resources as key inputs to the process of value creation to an effective training is a good way to bring successful innovation to the organization. Because after a big improvement in managerial processes, the organizations would need motivation and ability, driven from human capital in order to create innovative ideas, develop innovative methods and build new business opportunities.

For example, IBM 's old kind of desktop computer product needs to be innovated to invent new kind of laptop computer product, its advantage is that the user can easy to bring the laptop computer to go to anywhere because it is not too heavy. Even, nowadays, it invents the iphone computer,it is one phone, but it has also computer functions. It can download any photos , documents, typing words, sending email. Hence, IBM's innovation is successful and it will continue to attempt to invent any kind of undiscovered new kinds of computer products to satisfy computer users' needs. If it has no one effective training department to train excellent computer professionals to help it to research and invent any kinds of unique computer products. IBM will be possible to be one failure business organization, if the other computer competitors, such as Apple computer can invent any new kinds of computer products in the future. So, one effective training departmen can provide new techniques to let trainees to attempt to mind any new ideas , innovates the old products' knowledge to change the new product's concept. Such as the computer product case, it is from the desktop computer stage, then to change the laptop computer stage, till to nowadays to change the iphone computer stage.

In computer industry case, all of these innovations, such as the computer organization needs have strategic human resource practices to affect the selection, capacities and behaviors of employees, e.g. programmer, computer handware and software engineers etc. computer professionals to achieve the computer organization's goals and to change them. So, each one of these computer professionals is playing a major role in necessary conditions, classify and conduct individuals towards innovative activities. So, it seems that an effective training department, internal variable factors can help the computer organization's computer professionals to improve their software and hardware program design techniques in order to innovate the computer's old computer design to change to new computer design product. Hence, when the computer organization owns one effective training department , then it can provide good creative ideas to let its computer professionals to bring new mind creative ideas. if their any new mind creative ideas are success to assist the computer organization to innovate new kinds of computer products to attract future new computer users' attention in order to attract their purchase choices. Then, the computer organization's overall sale performance will be raised. It is due to the proficient and excellent computer professional's computer invention skillful level are raised from their trainers' training provisions. Thus, it seems that an effective training department can improve some organizations' overall sale performance in possible.

Secondly, I shall discuss how and why the recruitment and selection factor may influence performance. Can an effective human resource management activity , such as job analysis, recruitment, selection and development which can influence organization's overall performance? I shall assume that if the organization has no effective job analysis then it will lead to poor selection to recruit the not best employees to serve its organization. It is vital for the managers to ensure all the workers are fairly paid and they work in the desired working environment. So, when the organization has poor job analysis, it will influence some employees feel workload and work difficulties, if the employees has low knowledge level and skillful to do the job, but her/his salary / wage is higher to compare another high or other high knowledge and skillful level staff/staffs. Then, the high knowledge and skillful staff /staffs will feel unfair, due to whose salary is / salaries are lower to compare her/him. Then, he/she will perform low efficiency or inefficiency or low productive behavior in order to complain whose manager's unfair treatment in whose department. So, it seems that poor job analysis will influence poor selection and unfair recruitment internal variable factor as well as it will influence the high knowledg and skillful employees to attempt to perform low productive behavior to achieve the inefficient performance aim. This situation is popular in manufacturing industry, when one factory whose one product manufacturing worker feel whose knowledg and skillful level is better than another worker, he/she can manufacture many good quality of products number to compare another worker's number every day. But, he/she knows the another worker's wage is higher than him/her, it is possible that due to he/she works long time in this factory or he/she and his/her manager relationship is good. Hence, he/she may feel unfair and it can cause he/she choose to produce products number in order to perform his/her complaint to whose manager or factory employee.

However, in fact, he/she has absolute effort to produce many product number to compare the another worker's number. However, when the factory manager discovers the excellent performance worker's productive efficiency is poor. He/she plans to make the decision on selling the given employee, it means that finding another new employee to replace him/her (unemploying him/her). So, the manger will do wrong decision, he/she only believes the employee's knowledge and technique level is poor to compare the others. The manager does not know the employee perform low productive behavior, he/she aims to complain to the manager himself/ herself for unfair treatment. So, if the manager finds the another new worker to replace the high performance worker. But the new worker's productive number can be improved to achieved the old high productive worker's performance. It will influence the factory's overall productive performance in long term.

Thus, it implies that the internal changing factors between the new and old workers or the variables on the factory workers' productivities should be analyzed as well as the number of the factory's workers in the affected manufacturing department in the factory. This phenomenon can as well as take place from within the factory when the factory's workers show a competent ability and therefore, needs promotion. Thus, it explains why that effection in job analysis internal variable factor will influence the more accurate selection and recruitment to the most right employee in order to avoid the high knowledge and high technical employees choose to perform low productive and inefficient behaviors to achieve aim to complain their dissatisfactory treatment from whose employer. Then, it will influence the organization's overall productive performance to be poor , due to the high knowledge and high technique of employees' low productive behavioral performance. Every one of their low productive behaviors can influence the organization's overall productive performance to be poor in long term. Thus, one ineffective job analysis, selection and recruitment , human resource strategic internal variable factor will influence the organization's overall productive performance to be poor in possible long term.

Thirdly, I shall discuss why and how the facility management environment internal variable factor can influence the organization's overall performance in possible. The main idea indicates that the HRM performance presumption is that HR practices affect the employees' attitudes and behaviors, which further affects the operational performance, such as productivity , quality and innovation . It can bring a positive or negative effect on the financial and market performance to the organization. However, in any small, medium and large size organizations, they must need workplace and facilities to let their staffs to work in the stable locations. If the organization's location is not comfortable to let many staffs to feel in long term, e.g. factory, office, working environment. It is possible to influence its staffs' emotion to be bad, due to they need often to work in the poor working environment. It affects the employees' emotions negatively, this includes increased work intensity, stress, burn out and ripple effects from work into private life. It has relationship to influence the organization's employee individual productivity or service performance between the organization's internal variable facility management environment and employee individual emotion. It seems that if the employee has good emotion, it will influence his/her efficiency to be raised, otherwise, if the employss has bad emotion, it will influence his/her efficiency to be reduced. However, I assume that any organization's facility management workplace environment will influence employee individual emotion to be good or bad, then it will bring consequence , such as how the employee perform to do his/her task to be better or worse. For example, in one school classroom, its size is small, it only allows to the 30 students maximum number . If there are students need to sit in the classroom every class. Then, it will be possible to cause some students feel uncomfortable to sit in the classroom.. Then, it will be possible to influence these feeling uncomfortable students' learning emotions to be negative or they can not concentrate on learning when they still need sit in this small size classroom. Even, if these are 50 students ,even more students , they will sit in this small size classroom. Thus, it will bring the consequence in possible, such as the increase poor negative emotion student number as well as the poor learning performance. Thus, it seems that school organization's classroom size and learning material supply facilities, e.g. tables, chairs, computers, library books number, etc. these any one of the school's internal variable facilities number supplying and learning classroom size, attending lecture hall size , library size etc. facilities management factors will influence the student's learning emotion. Even the school's teachers' teaching emotions will be also influenced, due to they also need to go to classrooms or lecture halls (learning workplaces) to teach their students in the school. If the school has good teaching facilities management environment to let teachers to feel. Then it will be possible to influence their teaching performance to be better. Otherwise, if the school has worse teaching facility management environment. Then, it will possible to influence their teaching performance to be worse . Hence, it implies that any organization's facilities management environment will be possible to influence its employees' emotions to be negative or positive as well as it can also influence their services or productive performances to be good or bad indirectly. For example, in one poor factory environment, the workers need to work in one without air conditioners working place to work. Although, their working environment has fans, but they still feel hot in summer to work. Then, this poor workplace will influence the high knowledge and technical level workers whose performances to be poor in summer to work , due to their good working emotions will be influenced to be bad, due to they need to often to work in this high temperature factory's stable workplace or this high temperature warehouse's stable workplace in summer.

Thus, whether the working place environment can let employees to feel comfortable or not comfortable to work. This internal variable facility management factor will influence employee individual emotion to be good or bad in order to cause efficiency or performance to be improved. Thus, the organization's internal workplace facility management factor will influence efficiency and performance indirectly.

The final factor is that whether the reward and performance management factor can influence performance. Can the organization provide effective reward and performance management strategy influence limiting productive efficiency and profitablity. An effective reward can follow the individual performance, it depends on whether his/her performance is poor average, high or excellent level in order to give the reasonable reward to the employee fairly.

It seems that when there is one employee feel the organization can provide reasonable and fair reward to him/her. Then, the limiting factor (the stable fixed or unchanging staff number) will be possible influenced to raise productive efficiency, due to many of them feel their organization can provide fair and reasonable reward to encourage them to raise efficiency in order to earn more extra tangible reward, e.g. increasing salary/wage amount, increasing extra welfare , or intangible reward, increasing promotion chance, appreciation, job satisfaction. There are many employees feel their organization can not provide reasonable or fair reward. Then, it won't be encouraged them to work hardly. They will produce inefficiently. Thus, it explains why two organizations have same number of high knowledge and skillful level employees. The one orgnization's overall efficiency can be raised absolutely. Otherwise, the another organization's overall efficiency can not be raised absolutely, even its overall efficiency will be poor in possible. It is possible due to that the organization has many employees feel it can provide reasonable and fair reward when the employee performs better, he/she can earn more reward. Otherwise, the employee can not perform better, he/she can not earn more reward. Anyway, the another organization has many employees, they feel it can not provide fair and reasonable reward to them. When they work hardly, they can not earn more reward. Then, they will be possible to reduce their productivity and inefficiency. So, unfair and unreasonable reward can not encourage them to work hardly. Even, they will perform poorly, they aim to achieve the same productive level to the low productive employees to satisfy the same reward level feeling. Thus, it explains why effective reward and performance management factor has relationship to encourage many efficient employees to raise productivity as well as improve organizational overall productive performance in possible.

In conclusion, above these psychological factors will influence how human resource performance to be either improved better or inefficient productivity. It depends on the organization's internal variable factors to influence any one staff individual performance effectively. So, any organizations ought consider how to achieve its human resource strategic plan in order to keep their staffs overall performance can not be influenced to be worse from any one of these internal variable factors.

What is efficient achievement of
technological inputs factor in
construction industry

What is organizational efficient raising actual mean? I shall indicate construction industry case to explain technological factor is the major factor to assist construction organization to raise efficiency. For construction industry example, improved productivity could be attributed to advances in and increased usage of information technologies, increased competition, due to globalization and changes in workplace and organizational structures.

For construction efficiency, the construction process can reduce waste in coordinating labor and in managing, moving and installing materials, loss avoidance. It can achieve efficient aim. The construction productive efficient concept can be defined efficiency improvements as ways to cut waste and labor. So, one construction organizational efficient achievement means that it implemented through the capital facilities sector, these activities would significantly advance construction efficiency and improve the quality, timeliness, cost effectiveness of projects in construction processes.

On construction industry technological factor influence hand, it can influence that construction productivity how well, how quality, and at what cost buildings and infrastructure can be constructured, directly affects prices for homes and consumer products and the robustness of the national economy. Construction productivity will also affect the outcomes of national efforts to renew existing infrastructure systems; to build new infrastructure for power from renewable to renew existing infrastructure systems; to build new infrastructure for power from renewable resources to develop high-performance " green building" and to remain competitive in the global market. If the construction organization expected to achieve effficient aim. It ought consider how to change in building design, construction and renovation and in building materials and materials recycling, will be essential to the success of national efforts to minimize environmental impacts, reduce overall energy use, and reduce greenhouse gas emissions.

However, construction industry analysts differ on whether construction industry productivity is improved by efficiency outcome. They indicate construction efficiency needs to reduce 25-50 percent waste in coordinating labour and in managing, moving and installing materials. This is the most minimum standard efficient achievement level to any construction organizations.

What are the factors influence efficiency to any construction organizations? An efficient construction task process is made possible by a range of information technological tools and applications, including computer-aided design and drafting, three and four dimensional visualization and modeling programs, laser scanning, cost-estimating and scheduling tools and materials tracking. So, high technological tool will assist to raise efficient construction process to any construction organizations. It can help them to shorten time and avoid materials waste and control cost effective estimation for any construction projects.

Effective use of interoperate technologies requires effective team cooperative processes and effective planning up front and this it can help overcome obstacles to efficiency created by process fragmentation. Interoperable technologies can also help to improve the quality and speed of any construction project related decision making, integrate processes, managing supply chains, sequence work flows, improve data accuracy and reduce the time spent on data entry, reduce design and engineering conflicts and the subsequent need for rework, improve the life-cycle management of buildings and infrastructure.

All of these factors will influence whether the construction organization can implement efficiency in success. For example, interoperable techcholgies include legal issues, data-storage capacities and the need for " intelligent " search applications to sort quickly through thousands of data elements and make real-time information available for on-site decision making. How to improve job-site efficiency through more effective interfacing of people, processes, materials ,equipment, and information. The job site for a large construction project is a dynamic place, involving numerous contractors, subcontractors, trades people and labors, all of whom must require equipment, materials and supplies to complete their tasks. So, they need to know how to manage activities and demands to achieve the maximum efficiency from the limited available resources. Time, money, and resources will have possible to be wasted when projects are poorly managed, causing workers to have to wait around for tools and work crews are not on-site at appropriate time or when supplies and equipment are stored in complexity or difficulty, requiring that they can be moved multiple time (time waste).

How to improve job site safety and improve the quality of projects, significantly cut waste? The use of automated equipment, e.g. for excavation and earthmoving operations, pip installation, concrete placement, and information technologies, e.g. radio-frequency identification tags for tracking materials personal digital assistants for capturing field data. These high technological tool can help any construction projects to raise efficiency to process improvements and the provision for real -time information for improved management at the job site.

Moreover, on mannal research and development tools hand, instead of data technological tools hand, any construction organizations also need to consider how to take a variety of forms: How to test field on a job site? How to arrange lecture shows in efficient way, seminrs, training and conference, and scientific laboratories time, human resource available arrangement, spending expenditure budget to finish. Moreover, effective performance mearements are enablers of innovation and of corrective actions throughout a construction project's life cycle. They can help any construction companies or organizations understand how processes led to success or failure, improvements or inefficiencies and how to use that knowledge to improve construction products , processes and outcomes of active projects.

The nature of construction projects, the industry itself, any construction organizations ought consider the construction working environment how to influence construction workers' emotions. For example, when the construction site is high levels, of noise, dust and airborne particles, adverse weather conditions,and other factors that can cause injuries and thereby reduce efficiency and productivity. New types of equipment can make an active physically easier to perform, easier to control, move precise , and safer for construction workers. Similarly, changes in materials can reduce the weight of construction components, make them easier to handle, move and install. Manufacturing building components off-site providers need more control conditions and allow for improved quality and precision in the fabrication of the component, One study that examined the relationship between changes in material technology and construction productivity based on 100 construction a related tasks, the study found that labor productivity for the same activity increased by 30 % at least when higher materials were used and labour productivity also improved when construction activites were performed using materials that were easier to install or were pre-fabricated. So, it seems material heavy can influence construction worker individual productive efficiency in site, if the material is higher , then the construction worker's productivity will be influenced to improve (Goodrum et al. 2009).

Thus, the factors influence construction organization's efficiency. It focuses on whether the construction firm applies how advanced construction technologies to assist its construction workers to work as well as whether its construction environment can let workers to feel safe to avoid life danger or accident occurrence. When the workers do not worry about whose life safety as well as they can apply advanced construction technology to assist them to work. Then, their productive efficiencies ought need to be improved easily. Thus, facility management and advanced technology will be the main factor to raise construction workers' efficiencies.

Can effective departmental communication
factor influence successful organizational
effective change

In any organizations, their staffs must need communication either between the supervisor and low level staff(s) or between the same level staff(s) himself/herself/themselves. Has it relationship between communication and organizational efficient change? Can effective communication bring advantages to improve effort of employees to raise productive efficiency and execute change strategies more effective? Does organizational efficient change depend on effective communication in overall organization from low to top level, or top to low level? Why does effective overall organizational communication raise efficiency?

It is possible to consider that poorly managed change communication results in rumors and resistance to let every employee to know whether he/she ought know how to do it in order to finish whose task efficiently and effective result aim. Otherwise, an effective communication can let the employee to understand whether he/she needs how to do it clearly. Then, he/she will be possible to finish his/her task efficiently. So, it seems that employee individual job satisfaction will bring positive (effective) organizational outputs or negative (ineffective) organizational outputs, when he/she can be often communicated either efficiently or inefficiently.

In one big organization, if every employee feels difficult to communicate daily. Then, it is possible to influence his/her low productive , or inefficient performance. So, managers, supervisors and low level staffs ought have effective communication between them. Communication can include writing communication,e.g. memos are needed to delivered between internal different departments or between external departments daily immedicately by the delivered staff. Because it will influence the department delivers what message to another department to know to be delayed if the memo can not delivered to the department on the day. Then, it may influence inefficiency. Communication can include oral or verbal. The supervisor or manager ought take hir/her low level staff how to do the task to be improved immediately if he/she feels that the staff her error. If he/she can't tell the staff to let him/her to know whether he/she ought need how to do to be better. Then, it will cause the employee does not know whether what his/her error is and he/she ought need how to review to change his/her error to be right or reasonable acceptance in order to satisfy her/his supervisor/manager's task need. So, it seems that effective communication can influence how the staff's performance indirectly. Due to his/her misunderstanding how to do whose task to be improved or better. Then, it will bring inefficiency outcome in possible.

Any organizations need to depend on achievement of efficiency and effectiveness of themselves staffs communication behaviors every day.

During the staffs' communication , they will face problems of different understanding of communication related issues. Communication is either thus, such as negative communication phenomena that must be prevented or avoided; examples of difficult communication channel unavoidable problematic phenomena within the organization; they result from person/personality communication problems of participants or as positive (creative) phenomena that enable the organization's development. For example: the both different departments or single department communicator(s) can present in possibility to active more effective communication participation and they can encourage creation of new and opportunities, as well as they can contribute significantly to introduction of changes; when they enable additional forms of either verbal/oral or writing form of memo or report communication. For example, when one marketing team needs to write a report to recommend new idea concerns hoe to promote the new product to the global market. If the marketing team member can cooperate to discuss easily. Then, they can communicate how to gather data to cooperate how to communicate to sale team members in order to achieve sale target easily. Hence, when the marketing team members can communicate to sale team members to give ideas to let them to know what their new marketing plan will be implemented in order to follow their marketing plan to prepare how to sell their firm's new products strategically. When the organization is large size, e.f. IBM computer organization , the marketing team members will need effective communication to sale team members if they expect to implement any new product market plan to promote to sell to global computer users more easily/ If the IBM large computer organization sale department members need to spend much time to contact marketing department members in person. Then, due to difficult communication problem causes their plan to implement the marketing promotion plan in long time. It seems that marketing and sale departments' staffs inefficient performance, it is due to ineffective communication between departments in possible.

Moreover, ineffective or different communication environment also causes individual conflicts impact organization in different ways(e.g. indirectly , directly) are of different importance to influence the organization's overall different department cooperation relationship to be poor (e.g. highly urgent communication matter, less important communication matter). They organization's different departments may not know whether what is the highly urgent matter needs to be dealt immediately and what is the less important matter does not need to be delat immediately of the organization's department staffs feel difficult to communicate, due to time management is poor causes the department staffs do not know whether the department staffs ought spend time to do the communication tasks with another department staffs in prior in order to let the another department staffs know how they ought to follow their demand to finish their task in short time cooperation efficiently. Thus, effective communication can help the organization to effectiveness present the level at which the organization achieves its goals , when its different department staffs can communicate to cooperate to work team work to finish effectively any tasks effectively and efficiently in short time. So, effective departmental communication can bring the limited staffs number the benefit, such as invested less efforts and less time input to help the organization to achieve the most maximum outcome output of its aims and goals of the organization. The effective communication concerns the staff's communication behavioral factor, e.g. (message content) inputs, (writing or verbal communication method) operations, and (how long time to finish the mission) outputs relation between the factors (internal, external departments).

In conclusion, when one organization has many different departments as well as many staffs who need to often cooperate to communicate how to do evey task together. Time management is one important successful factor to every department individual staff, he/she needs to know whether what is the highly urgent important messages are needed to be communicated to let the another department staffs to know, that is the less important messages are needed to be communicated to the another department staffs to know. Hence, effective communication is concerned how the employee arranges time to work daily. If the employee is one poor time management person, then his/her communication will ineffective, the consequence will bring the organization's different departments' cooperation inefficiency ,even it can cause the organization's overall productive performance to be poor, due to long term inefficient departmental difficult communication between departments factor.

Can human resource development training
factor influence organizational productive
performance

Can HRD has relationship efficiency of HRD training and development in organization growth? HRM is the function within an organization that focused on recruitment of management of and provision of direction to people who work in the organization, performance measurement and rewarding management of effective HRM enables employees to contribute effectively and productivity to the overall company direction and the achievement of the organization's goals and objectives in possible.

How any why effective HRD can influence organizational efficiency? HRD is administrative activities with HR planning , recruitment , selection, training , appraisal , motivation, reward strategic focuses on employees. So employees are any organization's assets. It assumes that when the organization's employees (assets) can be trained effectively. Then, the assets (employees) efficiencies will raise in long term. HRM designs the effective activities to be arranged to provide to every employee individual task and coordinates , all human element within the organizations. When, every employee individual effort can be attributed to the most maximum . Then, it assumes the organizational overall efficiency will be raised. So, effective training is one suggestive method aims to raise employee individual effort level to the maximum. Then, the organization's overall efficiency will be raised in possible. However, HRD of training needs to be spent much money to invest in large size organizatons. Although, large size organizations, e.g. IBM computer firs, its training provides to spend much expenditure to train computer programming staffs to teach them how to create different new softwares in order to raise its competitive effort, it is long time investment value to its computer programming staffs because it is possible that it can upgrade its computer programming staffs' creative programming skills to be invented any new kinds of software products or designing new kinds of computers to sell. Hence, IBM 's HRD in training function has difficult evaluation its future human element of programming staffs' worth in long term. When, its programming staffs' skills can be upgraded to create special software products. Then, its overall staffs' efficient performance will also be raised because their software creative skills have been improved, due to effective training provision.

Effective training can solve the challenges of lack of skilled labour, heavy competition among firms, technological problems, low productivity and poor product implementation when placing a serious limitation on product expansion and increase in productivity. So, effective training needs have these characteristics: The trainer needs have good teaching skills or methods to raise employss individual creative effort, the training's content must need useful to satisfy the trainees' task need. So, the HRD's factors, such as organizational culture, job satisfactin, training and development and stress will have close relationship to influence the organization's overall employee productive performance or efficiency to be raised. For IBM computer example, it's organizational culture is that encouraging different department computer professionals create themselve software designing effort, providing effective training courses to raise their software designing creative effort in order to raise efficiency to achieve how to create new softwares in short time efficiently. Then, their job satisfaction may be increased, due to they feel that their software creative efforts and writing programming skillsa re raised or improved. Their stress will be also reduced, due to they do not need to worry about when they can create any new kinds of softwares or computer engineering systems to be invented to sell. So, if the IBM's HRD 's training function is one effective training course, it can assist IBM's programmers to raise their software and hardware creative effort to achieve raising IBM organization's overall productive performance and every software and hardware employee individual efficiency is also raised in possible.

Hence, any organization's training (HRD) will be one successful factor to influence the firm's productive performance and efficiency in possible. An organization's HRD of training and development function concerns with organizational activity aimed at improvement of organizational performance, including employee development, human resource learning and development. Training has traditionally been defined as the process by individuals change their skills, knowledge, attitudes, and/or behavior. Similarly, training involves designing and supporting learning activities that result in a desired level of performance. In constrast, HRD refers to long-term growth and learning, directing attention more on what an individual may need to know or do at some future time. In fact, training focuse more on current job duties or responsibilities, development points to future jon responsibilities. It emphasizes either the product of training and development or how individuals perform as a result of what they have learned.

However, an effective training is real an educational process, trainees can learn new information, re-learn and re-improve existing knowlege and skills , and more importantly have time to think and consider what new options can help them improve their effectiveness and performance at work in possible. Effective trainings are taught useful information that inform employees and develop skills and behaviors that can be transferred back to the workplace. The goals of training is to create an impact to cause the consequence , such as inefficiency can be changed to efficiently as well as ineffectiveness can be changed to effectiveness of the training itself's final goal. An effective training, the focus is on creating specific action steps and commitments that focus trainee's attention on incorporating their new skills and ideas back at work. However, training can be offered as skill development for individuals and groups. In general, trainings involve presentation and learning of content as a means for enhancing skill development and improving workplace behaviors.

These are both processes, training and development are often closely connected. Training can be used as a method for developing or improving or creating or upgrading skills and expertise to prevent problems from arising and can be an effective tool to reduce the performance gaps among staff . Training learning development can be used to create solutions to workplace issues, before or after the trainee had encountered any problems when they are working. Hence, an effective human resource training development can help the organization's overall employees on a team, in a department and as part of an institution identify effective strategies for improving performance. Also, it means that when the organization's employees overall performances are improved or efficiencies are raised, it may be concerned to an effective training is provided to teach them before in possible. It implies that how to measure whether the training is effective, it is decided by whether the organization's overall efficiency is raised or not. If the organization's employees overall productive performance whom are improved. Its efficiency is raised, then it is possible that it had implemented an effective training to provide them to learn useful knowledge to raise their creative effort to solve their job-related problems in possible.

Thus, it seems that it has relationship between training and efficiency to any organizations. HRD process aims to find ideas and solutions that can effectively return the group to a state of high performance. Training and HRD describes the formal, ongoing efforts that are made within organizations to improve the performance and the employer self-fulfillment of himself/herself through a variety of educational methods and programmes. Hence, in the modern workplace, training development process indicates that the trainer needs to teach from short term specific job skills to long term professional development.

All of above issues, they are based on these assumptions , such as these relationships: There is a relationship between organizational culture and employee performance, there is a relationship between job satisfaction and employee performance, there is a relationship between stress and employee performance as well as there is a relationship between training and development and employee performance. However, training and development is the main factor to improve employee performance. When the organization has effective training and development to provide to its employees (trainees) to learn , then their stress will be influenced to reduce, job satisfaction can b raised and they can accept to adapt their organizational culture more easily. Then, their efficiencies will raise more when they can perform better or improve performance between to compare their prior work performance in their organizations. Hence, training and development element will be the most influential element to compare the other organizational culture, job satisfaction and stress elements in a human resource management factor, which can influence whole firm performance (every employee individual performance) obviously. Because I assume when the organization can have an effective training and development deparrment to provide any kinds of effective training courses to let its employees (trainees) to learn. Then, it is possible that it can help all employees (trainees) to increase themselves confidence to work more easily. Due to an effective training development can influence they can accept more easier adaption to their organizational culture, bring more job satisfaction, when they feel more easier to do their tasks and their stress will also be reduced, when their any job-related difficulties will be solved every day. The final consequence will being that the organization's every employee (trainee) whom efficiency will be raised in possible as well as it will bring the firm's overall employees performances to be raised or improved or the firm itself overall performance to be raised or improved.

In conclusion, it seems that an effective training and development can assist the organization's employee(trainee) individual efficiency to be raised or improved, then it can assist the firm itself overall employees(trainees) whose performace to be raised or improved, due to the effective training can influence the trainees overall efficiency to be raised or improved, then it can influence the firm itself overall performance to be raised or improved in possible.

Factors influence employee motivation
to achieve organizational effective
performance

In fact, one organization can influence employee motivation, instead of external fairly management workplace environment, effective training provision better reward attractive strategies, fair performance measurement policy, accurate selection and recruitment interview method factors. The intrinsic factors that are also importance to influence employee motivation. For example, employee achievement and recognition work itself satisfaction, role and responsibility itself, salary structure, the level to which the employee feels appreciated and the building good or bad relationship between the employee and his/her supervisor or manager. There are influential psychological factor to impact on the employee performance in the organization.

Motivatin is the personal intrinsic emotion factor how to influence the employee to develop a certain mind set regarding his/her job. In fact, the exterinsic factors in the organization's human resource management practices particularly to ensure that the employees are influenced well motivated to perform their tasks. In addition, the organization may need extrinsic factors, such as encouraging employee involvement in the decision making participation and innovation in the decision making participation and innovation and increases the promotion appreciation or effective or useful training opportunities for the personal growth: It can positively influence the intrinsic factors of employee motivation.

Similarly, when one employee feels he/she acknowledges his/her role in important to influence on organizationa; effectiveness in order to assist the organization to overcome challenges, it can create a strong and positive job cooperation relationship with its employees as well as improving task fulfillment and ensure they have job satisfaction. In special, any large size organizations, they have low, middle and top level staffs. If they only feel the middle and high level management staffs too feel their roles are important , but they neglect to let the low level staffs, e.g. workers, clerks , salespeople, teacher etc. low level staffs. These staffs themseleves can also feel their roles are important in their organizations. Then, these large size organizations' effectiveness or efficiency or performance will be poor, due to these large size organizations feel they are not important staffs and they can be replaced from other new employees any time easily. Then, these low level staffs will have plan to find another organization (new employee) to replace their current employers any time. In the consequence, the organizations will be possible to lose any one of these important low level high efficient or good performance staffs (workers) or main HR asset. It will lead to failure of these organizations when these high efficient staffs (workers) high staff turnover number is increasing. The reason is because they feel that they hace hgh efficiency, so they can another new job very easily. So they have poor job satisfaction, due to their orgaizations can not motivate their low level staffs take more reward and good salary to attract them to work efficiently. These emplers do not understand the benefits of motivation in the workplace, then the investment in these low level employee related policies ca be easily justified. They only consider to satisfy the middles and top level managemet staffs' tasks need and reward need. If these low level employees are motivated to fulfill their tasks and achieve their goals, e.g. the organization's salespeople don't attmept to help their organization to sell their products hardly, the school's teachers do not attempt to find good teaching behavioral method to attract their students to raise interest to learn or let they feel fun to learn from their teaching in classrooms. Then, their poor sale or teaching performance will bring the students or product buyer number to be reduced. For this reason, it is essential for a manager/supervisor to understand what really motivates the low level employees without making on improvemen performance or inefficiency or low productive assumption.

Motivation means an individual's intensity, mind set, direction and spending effort toward attaining a goal. It can be either individual goal motivation to achieve any matter or visiion from personal benefit or the organization goal motivation to persuade its employees to help it to achieve its improvement performance, raising profit, raising sale , raising productive growth, raising efficiency , vison or aim . In this chapter, I shall discuss how the organization's motivation to employees can impact organization's overall performance or efficiency or productivity to be either good or bad. So, motivation to employees can include extrinsic motivation, e.g. increasing salary level, increasing welfares, as well as intrinsic motivation , e.g. job satisfaction, appreciation, promotion chance/ opportunity, feeling important role. I shall assume that if the employee lacks motivation emotion to work, then he/she will only spend less effort, nervous , time to attribute to work more hardly in the organization. Because they do not feel enjoyable to work , they won't raise efficient work performance, as well as their intrinsic motivation can not energize personal enjoyment, interest, or pleasure to let them they feel, they play one important role to earn unfair external reward to compare other same level or not same level staffs, e.g. the top level manager feels he/she earns unfair reward to compare another top level manager or the low level worker feels that he/she earn unfair reward to compare another low level worker, or the low level staff feels his/her organization gives excellent reward to the middle level or top level manager/supervisor only. So, it implies that the poor motivateion will occur to the overall organizational low middle and/or top level staffs , it is not only occur to the low level staffs. For example, if the organization's CEO feels his/her reward treatment is poor or unfair to compare to other companies' CEP reward. It means that it is possible that the organization's poor motivation or effort can be caused by the top, middle or low level staff, he /she needs to compare to othe companies; same level staff reward in general job market reward structure. Hence, any one organization needs to consider whether its reward is poor to compare other organizations' rewards. They can not only consider whether its reward is fair treatment to the low to to[level staffs issue only, but it neglects to consider whether wha tis the current market reward structure to its same competitors' rewards. It seems that one organization's employees will be possible compare whether their rewards are fair between themselves in their organizations as well as they will be possible compare whether their rewards are fair to the similar sale or service organizations or competitors. Hence, fair and reasoable reward can motivate or encourage every staff to accept to spend more effort, time, nervous to attribute to serve his/her organization.

Consequently, when the staff has good motivation, it may bring better efficiency, improving performance, raising productivity in possible. Otherwise, when the staff has bad emotivation, it may bring poor efficiency, or inefficiency, worse performance, reducing productivity in possible. So , it seems that it has indirect relationship between motivation and the organization's overall performance.

Performance measurement influences
effectiveness

Performance means understanding as achievement of the organization in relation with its set goals. It may include outcomes achieved, or accomplished through contribution of individuals or teams to the organization's strategic goals. It brings this question whether effective performance measurement can raise the organization's effectiveness.

Performance has a linkage with the individual potential and how best it is realized by the individual organization needs performance measurement because it needs to measure every employee individual job behavior in order to evaluate whether his/her performance is acceptable to either raise salary/wage or keep the same level salary/wage or appreciate to promote higher or senior position or unemploy (fire) the employee, when his/her performance is poor or unacceptable task level to earn this position level's reward with regard to manage. The employee's potential becomes the input to the productive process and performance is the out. It seems that when the one organization has many good performance employees number, then its effectiveness can not be improved to be better to compare the another similar industry organization has less good performance employees number , then its effectiveness can not improve to be better. The actua reason many include any company is one cooperative organization, it needs different teams or departments' members , workers, staffs to participate to work in low, middle, top level organizational structure. Hence, one organizational behavior can not be influenced only by one employee individual behavior or performance. The organization's overall performance or effectiveness ought be influenced by group (team) and organizational purpose, group (team) or organization capacities and resources, human climate in the group or team or the organization, the (team) group every member personal performance quality, efficient level , productive level. So, organization needs to consider how to make reasonable or fair feedback on group (team) overall performance. It does not only consider how to make reasonable or fair feedback on the top or middle level management employee individual performance only and it neglects to consider the low level employee individual performance measurement.

There are three abilities in an individual are said to be essential for performance achievement to evaluate whether the employee individual performance to excellent , good, common, poor level. They include the employee individual desire or motivation himself/herself ability, knowledge or know-how quality or action to actualize ability. Hence, one excellent performance employee whom ought have these above personal quality or ability characteristics, then he/she can perform the esscellent job performance. If the team or group or department owns the employees whom own above these abilities , then group, team, department's effectiveness will be improved, or efficiency can be raised, or productive growth can be raised more easily. However, effective performance measurement model was based mainly on financial measures and considered as one component of the planning and control cycle view, it is based on multipl non financial measures where performance measurement acts as an independent process includes in a set of activities.

How to design an effective performance measurement ? I shall assume that it has relationship between organizational effectiveness and performance measurement, also it means that whether organization is either effective or ineffective, it depends on whether its performance measurement is effective or ineffective. In essence, an organizational effectiveness represents the outcome of organizational activities when performance measurement consists of an assessment tool to measure effectiveness. In fact, the team " performance" and " effectiveness" are used interchangably because any organizational problems are related to their definition, measurement and explanation when their different groups, teams or departments' staffs are encountering the similar or same general problems when they are feeling in their departments. It seems that any organizations need to find whether what kinds of task problems to influence its different teams feel difficult to work , different department's staffs whom are feeling in general. Then, when the organization cna ensure whether what kinds of taxk problems that its staffs are facing. It can let its staffs to know how any why it needs its any ony one of its staffs to suggest useful ideas or opinions to help it to solve its organizational tasks problems in themselves department. If any one staff can know that whether he/she ought need how to do to solve whom task difficulty and the organization can attempt to use whose opinion to confirm his/her opinion is effective or useful to help it to solve his/her department general problems to its this department 's staffs' facing. Then, the organization can make more accurate judgement or evaluation to ensure the staff can be one excellent performance employee because he/she can attempt to find the effective or useful method(s) to help him/her deparment or team or group to solve his/ her department overall member whom are facing or encountering general task difficulties or problems that they feel needs to solve immediately. It seems that one excellent performance employee needs own have one unique difficult solvable ability that the other members can not find the effective or useful solution method(s) to help the department to solve. Its overall daily task difficulties that its department members can not solve easily. Similarly, it means that effective or fair performance measurement is based on whether the employee can find the best solution(s0 to help whom department to solve any task problems(difficulties) when it's overall members feel whom are encountering the same problems daily. When the department has one staff whom can suggest the best opinion(s) to help the department's staffs to raise efficiency or improve productivity to achieve whose department overall performance effectiveness to be improved better. Then the department staff ought be the excellent performance staff and his/her reward must be the best to compare other same level staffs in the department. Hence, the fair or reasonable performance measurement is based on the employee individual ability, it is not based on the department overall ability. It means that one department, however, its department structure level is the low, middle or top level, even the low level department ought have one or some staff(s) whom own personal ability is above to compare the same job responsibility level staffs in the department. The owninf above-average ability staff(s) ought earn more appreciation or promotion opportunity increasing to compare the owning low-average ability staffs in the department. When the department's low-average or general ability staffs who had been working in the department long time acknowledge why the staff(s) can be appreciated to promote to do the senior position or increase salary immediately to compare themselves. Then they will be influenced by the owning above-average ability of employee(s) to work hardly or attempt to find any solution(s) or method(s) to help themselves to solve any unpredictive task difficulties in order to achieve appreciation or increasing salary or senior position promotion personal aim or desire. Then, they can influence the department's overall effectiveness to be improved in long term possible. Hence, it seems to explain one effective or good performance measurement can influence the organization's effectiveness to be improved successfully.

An effective performance measurement model needs have an effective is measured in the terms of accomplishment of the outcomes to every department, it do not neglect the importance to review its error to help its different departments to solve themselves difficulties when their any one employee individual opinion is failure or unsuccessful to help it solve whom department's prior problems, also every employee ought have chance to let himself/herself to express opinions to let it to know whether what task difficulties when he/she is possible to encounter, and it ought let every department staff has opportunity to carry on group meeting discussion how to solve himself/herself department's overall facing general problems as well as it also needs to adopt the different solutions to attempt to find which one solution is the best in order to evaluate whether whom ability is above to any one in the department. It aims to make the more accurrate performance measurement decision to give the fair and reasonable reward or welfare to any one in any department.

In conclusion, an effective performance measurement has these requirements: It needs to find whom the employee(s) has/have good decision making ability to help himself/herself department ot the other employees to solve general task difficulties in order to improve of decision process though (setting performance and strategies goals and ensuring an adequate level and mix of resources) and coordination to parts of a business to achieve objective; it needs have effective control to feedback to ensure the input-process-out system. Input means that different reward structure to be designed to the low , middle and top level employees' performance measurementevaluation and reward evaluation need, process means that an effective employee performance measurement evaluation startegic system and ouput means that an fair and reasonable reward structure implementation to every low, middle and top level employee. It is properly and to motivate and evaluate employees, managers need and it also needs to consider the overall organization how is related to its values, preferences and where themsleves department employees should be focusing their attention and energy how to attempt to solve solve themselves task difficulties in order to find whom is/are the above -average ability employee(s) in themselves department and to be recommend to appreciate to earn the more fair and reasonable reward immediately. So, an effective performance measurement organization is not only composed of individuals, but also interdependent groups with different immediate goals, (desired from specializations), different ways of working , different formal training and even different personality types. For example, staffs who work in accounting department , often have every different personality, goals , training and styles of work and socialization than staffs who work in advertising or marketing departments. So , the organization ought need to follow whether the staffs are working in which departments in order to arrange the most reasonable job task responsibilities to let him/her to work. It means that one accounting deparment will need to employ different accounting skillful staffs to do these different accounting task functions, such as financial and finance function, salary and performance measurement calcuation function, cost accounting and management budget function. So, if one employee whom is proficient on financial accounting, but he/she is arranged to do the management and cost budget function task duties. Then, it will influence whom performance to be poor, due to he/she is not proficient do do management and cost budget analysis task duties. Although, he/she has accounting knowledge and working experiences, but it does not mean that he/she has ability to do management and cost budget task duties better in the accounting department. So, any manager needs to select the right employee to arrange the right task function to let the employee do the right task responsibility duties in his /her department. If the manager selected the wrong employee to be arranged him/her to do the wrong job task reponsibility position in whose department. It is possible to influence its department's overall efficiency or productive performance to be poor.

Hence, it has close indirect relationship between performance measurement and the organization's overall effectiveness. Because effectiveness oriented companies are concerned with output, sales, quality, creation of value added, innovation, cost reduction. It measures the degree to which a business achieve its goals or the way outputs interest with the economics and social environment. When the organization has an effective or fair and reasonable performance measurement strategy. Then, its employees will feel more satisfactory to improve productive performance or efficiency in order to earn more reasonable awards easily. When the organization has many employees can improve their productive efficiency. Then, its overall productive number will be increased or service performance will be improved . Consequently, its effective performance can be also improved, thus it explains why and how when one organization has one effective performance measurement strategy , it can improve its organizational overall performance to be more effective because every department will have more employees whom like to attribute more nervous, effort, time to do themselves job duties in order to achieve appreciation, promotion, increasing salary opportunity when they acknowledge their organization has fair and reasonable performance mangement policy to evaluate themselves performance fairly.

Similarly, in one fair and reasonable performance measurement organizaional workplace environment, it will influence every department employee individual emotion to be positive, he/she can feel whom need to spend more effort, tiem and nervous to work in order to assist his/her department to raise efficiency or productivity or improve service performance aim. Then, if the organization has many department's efficiency and productive growth can be raised. It means that the organization's overall performance can be more effective also. So, it has indirect relationship between performance measurement and organizational overall performance.